# A WALK THROUGH SAN FRANCISCO, CALIFORNIA 2023: A TRAVEL GUIDE

The Tourist's Handbook to 100 + Experiences; Eating, Sleeping, and Sightseeing in The City by the Bay

Amber Romero

# COPYRIGHT

# TABLE OF CONTENTS

# INTRODUCTION

## Welcome to San Francisco

Welcome to the amazing world of San Francisco, where eclectic charm, vibrant culture, and jaw-dropping views await you! In the pages of "A Walk through San Francisco, California: Your Handbook to Eating, Sleeping, and Sightseeing in the City by the Bay," get ready for an adventure like no other. It's time to dive into the heart and soul of this iconic city and discover all its hidden treasures hidden amidst the mysterious fog-filled streets.

Prepare your taste buds for an explosion of flavors as you indulge in the tantalizing culinary delights that San Francisco has to offer. And fear not, tired traveler, because we've got your back! Find the coziest sanctuaries to rest those weary feet and recharge your energy for the next thrilling escapade.

But wait, there's more! Immerse yourself in the awe-inspiring sights that will leave you breathless and fuel your imagination. Our comprehensive handbook is the ultimate sidekick, filled with invaluable insights, practical tips, and a curated selection of must-see spots. With our guidance, each step you take in the city will become an unforgettable experience that you'll cherish forever.

Picture this: You step off the plane, full of anticipation and excitement, ready to experience the city that has captured the hearts of so many. You can't help but feel a little nervous - after all, San Francisco is known for its vibrant culture, stunning architecture, and unique history. You've heard so much about the Golden Gate Bridge, Fisherman's Wharf, and the bustling streets of Chinatown. But what else is there to see and do in this enchanting city?

From the first steps onto the streets of San Francisco, you'd be immediately hit by the energy and charm of the city. The air is thick with the aroma of fresh seafood and sourdough bread, and the sounds of street performers fill your ears. You'd look up and see the iconic cable cars making their way up and down the steep hills, and you can't help but smile in wonder.

While San Francisco is a city of sights and sounds, It's also a place of history and culture, a place that has captured the hearts of so many people from all around the world. From the vibrant neighborhoods of the Mission and Castro to the stately mansions of Pacific Heights, there's a lot of special highlights in this city by the bay.

So come along with me on a journey through the vibrant streets of San Francisco. Let me show you the best places to eat, sleep, and sightsee, and introduce you to the unique culture and history of this amazing city. It doesn't matter if you're a first-time visitor or a seasoned traveler, I promise you'll fall in love with San Francisco, just like I did. Let's explore!

## Why Visit San Francisco?

Did you know that San Francisco is home to the oldest Chinatown in North America? That's right - this vibrant neighborhood has been a hub of Chinese culture and tradition since the 1800s. From the colorful pagoda roofs to the delicious dim sum, Chinatown is a must-visit destination for any San Francisco tourist.

Did you know that San Francisco has a unique characteristic weather pattern? Locals have given it the nickname "Karl," and it refers to the fog that often blankets the city, especially during the summer months. Nobody knows for sure where the name came from, but it's believed to have been popularized by the @KarltheFog Twitter account. Yep, you heard that right! This hilarious Twitter account personifies the fog and gives updates on its whereabouts around the city. While Karl may sometimes obscure the view of San Francisco's landmarks including the Golden Gate Bridge, many locals see it as a defining feature of the city's climate and embrace it with open arms.

San Francisco is also home to the crookedest street in the world - Lombard Street. This steep, winding road is famous for its eight hairpin turns, and is a popular destination for visitors looking for a unique photo opportunity.

If you're a fan of the iconic Golden Gate Bridge, then you might be surprised to know that it was actually painted orange to help it stand out in the fog. And speaking of fog, did you know that San Francisco is one of the foggiest cities in the world? That's why you should always bring a jacket when you visit - even in the summer!

San Francisco is also a city of innovation - it's home to some of the world's most famous tech companies, including Apple, Google, and Facebook. But did you know that the first computer mouse was invented in San Francisco? That's right - the prototype was created by a man named Douglas Engelbart in the 1960s.

Finally, if you're a fan of sourdough bread, then you'll be happy to know that San Francisco is famous for its sourdough. The unique flavor of the bread is thanks to a particular strain of wild yeast that can only be found in San Francisco. So make sure you try a sourdough bread bowl filled with clam chowder while you're here - it's a San Francisco classic!

Did you know that San Francisco has one of the coolest Japantowns in the whole US? That's right! In fact, there are only two other Japantowns in the entire country, and they're in San Jose and Los Angeles. That's why Japanese culture is such a big deal around here, and why San Francisco has an amazing Japanese Tea Garden that you just have to see.

# CHAPTER ONE

## Getting to Know San Francisco

### The History of San Francisco

San Francisco has seen its fair share of triumphs and tragedies, but always manages to rise above it all. It truly is a city full of adventure, innovation, and resilience.

San Francisco's history began in 1776, when a group of Spanish explorers discovered a natural harbor on the coast of California. They named it Yerba Buena, which means "good herb" in Spanish, because the area was covered in a fragrant herb called sweet fennel.

In the mid-1800s, the city underwent a massive transformation when gold was discovered in California. Thousands of people flocked to San Francisco in search of fortune, creating a booming economy and a diverse population.

But the city faced its fair share of challenges as well. In 1906, a devastating earthquake and subsequent fire destroyed much of San Francisco, leaving over 200,000 people homeless. But San Franciscans are a resilient bunch, and they quickly set to work rebuilding their city. Within a few years, San Francisco had been completely rebuilt and was once again thriving.

During World War II, San Francisco played a crucial role in the Allied effort. It was the departure point for thousands of troops and supplies headed for the Pacific Theater, and it was also the site of the signing of the United Nations charter in 1945.

In the 1960s, San Francisco became known as the center of the counterculture movement. The Haight-Ashbury neighborhood was a hub of hippie activity, and iconic events like the Summer of Love and the Human Be-In cemented San Francisco's place in pop culture history.

Today, San Francisco remains a beacon of innovation and progress. It's home to some of the world's most famous tech companies, as well as a thriving arts and culture scene. From the Golden Gate Bridge to the steep hills and cable cars, San Francisco is a city full of character and charm, a city that will always capture the imagination and inspire awe.

## Geography of San Francisco

San Francisco is a city located in the northern part of California, on a peninsula that juts out into the Pacific Ocean. It's surrounded by water on three sides, with the San Francisco Bay to the east and the Pacific Ocean to the west and south.

The city is known for its steep hills, which can make for a challenging (but rewarding!) workout if you're exploring on foot. The most famous of these hills is Nob Hill, which is home to some of the city's most luxurious hotels and stunning views.

One of the most iconic landmarks in San Francisco is the Golden Gate Bridge, which spans the entrance to the San Francisco Bay. It's a suspension bridge that's over a mile long, and its bright orange color makes it easily recognizable.

San Francisco is also home to a number of parks and green spaces, including Golden Gate Park and the Presidio. These areas offer a chance to escape the hustle and bustle of the city and enjoy some peace and quiet in nature.

The city is divided into different neighborhoods, each with its own unique character and charm.

Finally, it's worth mentioning that San Francisco is located on the San Andreas Fault, which is a major geological fault line that runs through much of California. While earthquakes are relatively rare, they are a part of life in San Francisco and a reminder of the city's geological history.

## Climate and Weather

First things first, let's talk about what you should expect when it comes to temperature. San Francisco has a relatively mild climate year-round, with temperatures rarely dropping below freezing or soaring above the mid-80s Fahrenheit. This is due in large part to the city's proximity to the ocean and the bay, which help to regulate the temperature.

That being said, there are some variations in temperature and weather patterns throughout the year.

The summer months (**June-August**) are typically the warmest, with average temperatures in the mid-60s to mid-70s Fahrenheit. However, it's important to note that San Francisco can be prone to something called the "marine layer," which is a layer of cool, damp air that can settle over the city and bring cooler temperatures and foggy conditions.

The fall (**September-November**) is often considered one of the best times to visit San Francisco, as the weather tends to be mild and pleasant. Average temperatures during this time are usually in the mid-60s to low 70s Fahrenheit.

Winter **(December-February)** is the rainy season in San Francisco, with the most precipitation typically occurring in January and February. While temperatures don't usually drop below freezing, it can feel quite chilly and damp during this time, with average temperatures in the mid-50s Fahrenheit.

Finally, spring **(March-May)** is another great time to visit San Francisco, with mild temperatures and relatively low rainfall. Average temperatures during this time are usually in the mid-60s to low 70s Fahrenheit.

So, when should you visit San Francisco? Well, it really depends on what you're looking for! If you want warm weather and lots of sunshine, then the summer months might be your best bet. However, if you prefer milder temperatures and fewer crowds, then spring and fall might be a better choice. And if you don't mind a bit of rain and cooler temperatures, then winter can also be a great time to visit.

## Culture and Lifestyle

San Francisco is a city like no other! It's known for its unique culture and lifestyle, which sets it apart from other cities in the United States. Imagine a place where diverse communities come together to create a melting pot of art, music, and food. That's San Francisco!

One of the most exciting things about San Francisco is its long history of activism and social justice. San Franciscans have always been at the forefront of fighting for equality and justice. The famous LGBTQ+ rights movement and the Black Lives Matter protests are just a few examples of how San Francisco is a city that stands up for what they believe is right.

Art and creativity are also a big part of San Francisco's culture. You'll find numerous art galleries, museums, and theaters showcasing everything from classical masterpieces to modern-day innovations. Whether you're into traditional art, street art, or avant-garde performances, you are sure to find something that suits you.

Now, let's talk about food! San Francisco is a foodie's paradise, and it's famous for its diverse and eclectic culinary scene. You can indulge in classic seafood dishes or try out fusion cuisine. With the city's many farmers' markets and specialty food stores, it's easy to sample the local fare and find something new to love.

Finally, San Francisco's relaxed and laid-back lifestyle is a major draw for visitors and locals alike. The people here tend to take things a little slower, and the city has a reputation for being one of the most open-minded and accepting places in the world. So come and experience the welcoming culture and lifestyle of San Francisco – it's an unforgettable place to visit.

## Geography of San Francisco

Welcome to the incredible world of San Francisco, the "City by the Bay"! This geographically captivating metropolis in northern California has it all: stunning landscapes, iconic landmarks, and even its own microclimates!

Spread across about 46.9 square miles (121 square kilometers), San Francisco is famous for its hilly terrain. Brace yourself for some unforgettable sights as you navigate its steep inclines like Lombard and Filbert streets, which offer breathtaking views of the cityscape.

San Francisco is surrounded by water on three sides! To the west, you have the mighty Pacific Ocean, while the north and east boast the beautiful San Francisco Bay. And let's not forget the world-famous Golden Gate Bridge, spanning the Golden Gate Strait and connecting the city to Marin Headlands. Don't miss the chance to snap some incredible photos and take in the panoramic vistas!

As you explore, you'll discover that San Francisco is a patchwork of distinct neighborhoods, each with its own personality. From the lively streets of Chinatown to the bohemian vibes of Haight-Ashbury, there's something fascinating everywhere in this diverse and vibrant city.

Now, here's a fascinating twist: San Francisco has microclimates! Thanks to its varied topography and the ocean's influence, different parts of the city can experience different weather patterns. You might find yourself wandering through the mysterious fog in the western and coastal areas, while the eastern and inland neighborhoods bask in sunny and warm skies. Talk about a weather adventure!

But wait, there's more to explore beyond the city limits! To the north, you can embark on an adventure through the breathtaking Marin Headlands, with its rugged cliffs, enchanting hiking trails, and intriguing historical sites. And to the south lies the world-famous Silicon Valley, a hub of innovation and home to countless tech companies.

Oh, and did we mention that San Francisco is perfectly situated near other fantastic destinations? A short drive away, you can dive into the renowned wine regions of Napa Valley and Sonoma, or soak up the stunning coastal beauty of the Big Sur coastline down south.

## Dos and Don'ts

- Do:

If you plan on driving in San Francisco, just a heads up that finding parking can be a bit of a nightmare and it can also be pretty expensive. But don't worry, there are some great alternatives. Public transportation in the city is awesome and can even be a fun way to explore. My recommendation would be to park your car at your hotel's lot or a long-term garage and then use public transportation or walk around until it's time to hit the road again. This way you won't waste precious time searching for a parking spot and save some money too.

Take a ride on the iconic cable cars. They're like no other mode of transportation you've ever experienced! Not only do they take you to all the hot spots around the city, but they're also a total adventure. To make the most of your trip, I suggest getting a pass that covers the days you'll be in town. That way you can easily hop on and off the cable cars without having to worry about buying individual tickets. You can grab your passes at the turnaround point, just beyond Union Square. Trust me, it's a must-do when in San Francisco.

Take a ride on the historic streetcars that run along the F line route! These streetcars come from all over the world and are each one-of-a-kind, like a 1928 Italian streetcar. Riding these streetcars is not only a unique experience, but it also gives your feet a break while you glide along the waterfront from the ferry landing to Fisherman's Wharf. Don't miss out on this opportunity to travel in style.

Book a ticket to Alcatraz Island. Even though it might seem odd to visit an old maximum-security prison while you're on vacation, trust me, it's totally worth it! You'll have an amazing time exploring "The Rock," and the tour even includes a boat ride on the bay, which is super cool. Just make sure to book your tickets in advance to ensure you get a spot on the tour. You won't regret it!

Explore the city's diverse neighborhoods: Each neighborhood in San Francisco has its own unique vibe and attractions, from the bustling streets of Chinatown to the colorful murals of the Mission District. Make sure to venture beyond the tourist hotspots and discover the hidden gems that make San Francisco so special.

Take public transportation: San Francisco's public transportation system is easy to use and affordable, with options like buses, trains, and cable cars. Plus, it's a great way to see the city without the hassle of driving and parking.

Dress in layers: San Francisco's weather can be unpredictable, so it's a good idea to dress in layers so you can adjust to the changing temperatures throughout the day. Don't forget a jacket, even in the summer!

Try the local cuisine: San Francisco is famous for its food, so be sure to sample the city's diverse culinary offerings. From seafood to sourdough bread to Mexican cuisine, there's so much to taste and relish..

- Don't:

Leave valuables in your car: Unfortunately, car break-ins are a common occurrence in San Francisco, so it's best to leave valuables at home or take them with you when you leave your car.

Forget your sunscreen: Even on cloudy days, the sun in San Francisco can be strong, so make sure to apply sunscreen to avoid getting burned.

Be loud and disruptive: San Francisco is a diverse and inclusive city, but it's important to be respectful of others and their personal space. Avoid being loud and disruptive in public spaces, especially at night.

Overlook safety: While San Francisco is generally a safe city, it's always important to be aware of your surroundings and take precautions to stay safe, especially at night or in unfamiliar areas.

# CHAPTER TWO

## Planning Your Trip

### Getting to San Francisco

If you're traveling internationally, you can fly directly to San Francisco International Airport (SFO) from major cities like London, Paris, Tokyo, Sydney, and more. Airlines like British Airways, Air France, Japan Airlines, and United Airlines offer direct flights to SFO, so check out their websites to find the best deals.

If you're traveling domestically within the United States, you have a few options. You can fly to SFO from almost any major city in the country, or you can take a road trip and drive to San Francisco. The famous Highway 1 runs right along the California coast, offering stunning views and plenty of stops along the way.

For those who prefer a more scenic route, you can also take the train. Amtrak's Coast Starlight train runs from Seattle to

Los Angeles, passing through San Francisco along the way. This is a great option if you want to see the beautiful California coastline without having to drive.

If you're traveling on a budget, you can consider taking a bus or a shuttle. Companies like Greyhound and Megabus offer affordable options for travel within the United States, while shuttle services like SuperShuttle and Go Lorrie's provide transportation to and from the airport.

## Visa and Papers

The visa requirements for San Francisco depend on your country of origin and the purpose of your visit. If you're a citizen of the United States, you won't need a visa to travel to San Francisco. But if you're coming from another country, you might need a visa depending on your nationality. The US has a visa waiver program for many countries, which means that visitors can stay in the US for up to 90 days without a visa.

To be eligible for the visa waiver program, you'll need to have a valid passport from a participating country, and you'll need to apply for an Electronic System for Travel Authorization

(ESTA) online. This is an online application that asks for basic information about yourself and your travel plans. The ESTA is valid for two years. Once you've been approved, you can enter the US as many times as you like during those two years, as long as you don't stay for more than 90 days at a time.

If you're not eligible for the visa waiver program, you'll need to apply for a visa. This process can take some time, so make sure to start early. You'll need to schedule an appointment at the US embassy or consulate in your country, and provide documentation such as a valid passport, proof of financial support, and a travel itinerary. The process involves filling out an application, providing documentation, and attending an interview at a U.S. embassy or consulate in your home country.

It's also important to note that all visitors to the US, regardless of whether they need a visa or not, will need to fill out a Customs Declaration Form when they arrive in the US. This form asks for information about the items you're bringing into the country, and whether you've visited any farms or been in contact with livestock.

For business travelers or those planning to study in San Francisco, you may need to apply for a different type of visa. It's always a good idea to consult with a visa specialist or the nearest U.S. embassy or consulate to get the most up-to-date information.

Remember, it's important to start the visa application process as early as possible, as it can take some time to get everything sorted out. But don't let that discourage you - San Francisco is an amazing city with so much to offer, and it's worth the effort to make your trip happen.

## Customs

The United States has strict customs regulations. You'll need to have your passport and any necessary visas or other travel documents ready for inspection upon arrival. You may also be asked questions about the purpose of your trip and the length of your stay.

As for duty-free items, travelers are allowed to bring certain items into the United States without having to pay duties or taxes. However, there are limits on the amount of duty-free items you can bring with you. For example, you can bring up to 1 liter of alcohol and up to $800 worth of merchandise without having to pay any duties or taxes. Anything over these limits may be subject to additional fees.

## Vaccinations

San Francisco has specific regulations in place for certain types of travelers. For example, if you are traveling from a country where yellow fever is endemic, you may be required to show proof of vaccination before entering San Francisco. Additionally, during the COVID-19 pandemic, travelers may need to show proof of vaccination or a negative COVID-19 test result to enter San Francisco. It's important to keep up to date with the latest travel restrictions and regulations to ensure a smooth entry into San Francisco.

# CHAPTER THREE

## Must-See Attractions

### Golden Gate Bridge

Golden Gate Bridge

The Golden Gate Bridge was completed in 1937 and has since become one of the most recognizable landmarks in the world. It spans 1.7 miles across the Golden Gate Strait, which connects the San Francisco Bay and the Pacific Ocean. It was once the longest suspension bridge in the world and is still one of the most impressive engineering feats ever achieved.

There are several ways to experience the Golden Gate Bridge, but one of the best ways is by walking or biking across it. The bridge has dedicated pedestrian and bike paths, which offer stunning views of the city skyline, the bay, and the ocean. You can rent bikes from various shops around the city and then take a leisurely ride across the bridge, taking in the views as you go.

If walking or biking isn't your thing, you can also drive across the bridge. There are several lookout points on either side of the bridge that offer stunning views, so make sure to stop and take some photos!

While the bridge itself is the main attraction, there are also several other things to do in the area. The nearby Presidio offers hiking trails, scenic overlooks, and historic sites, while the quaint town of Sausalito on the other side of the bridge is worth a visit for its charming shops and restaurants.

Getting to the Golden Gate Bridge is easy. If you're driving, there's a parking lot on the San Francisco side of the bridge. You can also take public transportation, such as the Muni bus or the Golden Gate Transit bus, which both have stops near the bridge.

Best Golden Gate Bridge Viewing Spots

- Battery Spencer

This is one of the most popular spots to take pictures of the Golden Gate Bridge, and it's not hard to see why. From this vantage point, you can see the entire bridge and the city skyline in the background. It's particularly beautiful during sunrise and sunset when the sky is painted with shades of orange, pink, and purple. Just make sure to arrive early to get a good spot!

- Baker Beach

Another great spot is Baker Beach. This beach is situated at the foot of the Golden Gate Bridge and offers stunning views of the bridge as well as the Pacific Ocean. It's a popular spot for picnics, swimming, and sunbathing. But be aware that parts of the beach are clothing-optional, so if that's not your thing, you might want to steer clear of those areas.

- Fort Point

For a more unique perspective, head to Fort Point. This historic site was used to defend the San Francisco Bay during the Civil War and is located right under the Golden Gate

Bridge. From here, you can capture the bridge from a lower angle, which makes for a really cool photo. You can also take a tour of the fort and learn about its history.

- Lands End

This rugged coastline offers stunning views of the Golden Gate Bridge from a distance. You can hike along the Coastal Trail and take in the breathtaking scenery, or head to the Sutro Baths ruins and capture the bridge in the background. It's a great spot to visit any time of day, but the golden hours of sunrise and sunset really make the view unforgettable.

## Alcatraz Island

Alcatraz Island

Alcatraz Island is known for its notorious prison that was in operation from 1934 to 1963. The island has a rich history and has been used for various purposes over the years, including as a military fortification, a military prison, and a federal penitentiary. Today, it is a popular tourist destination and is managed by the National Park Service.

To get to Alcatraz Island, you need to take a ferry from Pier 33 in San Francisco. It's a quick and easy ride, and the views of the city skyline and the Golden Gate Bridge from the ferry are spectacular.

Once you arrive on the island, you can explore the prison, take guided tours, and learn about the lives of the inmates who were housed there. The audio tours are particularly popular and provide a great way to learn about the history of the prison in an engaging and interactive way.

Aside from the prison, Alcatraz Island is home to a variety of wildlife, including birds, sea lions, and even the occasional whale or dolphin. There are also beautiful gardens and breathtaking views of the city skyline and the Golden Gate Bridge.

In terms of exploring the island, we recommend wearing comfortable shoes and dressing in layers, as the weather can be unpredictable. Be sure to bring your camera to capture the stunning views, especially during sunset and sunrise.

## Alcatraz Island Essential Information

If you plan on arriving at the Pier by car, it's important to note that parking near Pier 33 can be a bit of a hassle. In fact, it may even be impossible to find parking in the area. And even if you do find a spot, there's usually a time limit on the parking meters. So, my advice is to look for parking a little further away from Pier 33.

The good news is that there are plenty of parking garages and public parking lots with no time limit that are just a quick 10-minute walk from Pier 33. If walking isn't your thing, you can also take a bus or even an old-timey tram to get to the pier.

You can only get your tickets through Alcatraz Island Tickets. Luckily, the tickets include a ferry ride to and from the island, so you won't have to worry about that.

They offer two tours: the day tour for $46 and the night tour for $53.

But listen up, tickets sell out fast, sometimes even weeks in advance. So, it's better to book them online up to 90 days in advance. And here's a pro tip: print out your tickets ahead of time, so you won't have to wait in line to pick them up at will-call. Trust me, this will save you tons of time and hassle.

Make sure to grab a bite before you head out to Alcatraz Island. While there is a cafe at the Pier, it's on the pricier side. Plus, you won't be able to eat or bring any food onto the island (except on the dock by the ferry). So, it's a good idea to come prepared with some snacks or a meal to keep you fueled up for the tour.

You'll need to have a photo ID with you in order to board the ferry. Don't forget to bring it.

Once you arrive at the island, make sure to catch the 15-minute short video. Trust me, it's a must-see, especially if you're not familiar with Alcatraz. The video is packed with fascinating info about the island and its penitentiary straight from former guards and inmates. Can you believe that the island has a rich military past and that Native Americans used to call it home? It's definitely worth watching!

Make sure to take advantage of the free audio tour. It's a game-changer. It's so informative and really helps you understand what you're seeing. The tour will take you through the penitentiary step by step, so you won't miss a thing. And the best part? You can pause it whenever you want! Plus, you'll hear from some of the previous guards and prisoners who share their experiences on the island. So don't miss out on this must-do activity. You'll be able to use the audio guide to track down the cells of famous former inmates like Machine Gun Kelly and Al Capone. Plus, you'll get to see where some infamous escape attempts took place! The audio guide will lead the way, so you won't miss a thing.

If you're a national parks enthusiast, you'll definitely want to bring your Passport To Your National Parks book with you to Alcatraz Island. It's part of the Golden Gate National Recreation Area, so you can get your book stamped there. But don't worry if you forget yours, the bookstore has one available for purchase. And the bookstore also sells a cool sticker sheet that includes stickers from all the sites in the Golden Gate NRA where passport stamps are available. This is a different sticker sheet from the yearly ones offered by the National Park Service, and it's a fun way to remember your trip.

## Fisherman's Wharf

Fisherman's Wharf is a lively waterfront area that dates back to the Gold Rush era of the 1850s. It was originally a hub for fisherman and crabbers, but has since evolved into a bustling tourist destination that's packed with things to see and do. Fisherman's Wharf is the stretch of land between Pier 39 and Ghirardelli Square, and it's pretty easy to get around by walking. But if you want to take a break from all the walking, you can hop on one of the cool vintage streetcars that run up and down the wharf.

Fisherman's Wharf

Fisherman's Wharf stretches from Pier 33 where you can catch a boat to Alcatraz, all the way to Fort Mason and the famous Ghirardelli Square. On the other side, it's bordered by some awesome neighborhoods like Nob Hill, Russian Hill, and Telegraph Hill. It's a pretty big area, but you can easily explore it all by walking along the waterfront or taking a streetcar.

Now, onto the best ways to explore Fisherman's Wharf. My recommendation is to take a leisurely stroll along the waterfront promenade, which offers stunning views of the San Francisco Bay and Alcatraz Island. You'll pass by charming souvenir shops, street performers, and historic ships like the

USS Pampanito submarine and the SS Jeremiah O'Brien Liberty Ship. For a more immersive experience, hop on a classic cable car or a historic streetcar that runs along the wharf.

The wharf is famous for its seafood, and you can find everything from fresh Dungeness crab to clam chowder in sourdough bread bowls. My personal favorites are the fish tacos at The Codmother Fish and Chips. If you have a sweet tooth, be sure to stop by the world-famous Ghirardelli Chocolate Factory for a delicious treat.

Animal lovers can visit the Aquarium of the Bay or take a boat tour to see sea lions lounging on Pier 39. History buffs can explore the Maritime Museum or take a guided tour of the USS Pampanito submarine. And thrill-seekers can get their adrenaline fix on the famous RocketBoat ride that speeds through the bay at high speeds.

Finally, let's talk about how to get to Fisherman's Wharf. If you're staying in San Francisco, it's easy to get there via public transportation like buses or streetcars. If you're driving, be aware that parking can be a bit challenging, so plan accordingly. I recommend arriving early in the day to beat the crowds and secure a good parking spot.

**Fisherman's Wharf Bucket List**

- Pier 39

Walking by Pier 39 is a must-do when in San Francisco! You'll get the chance to see a bunch of adorable sea lions hanging out on the docks. They've been there since an earthquake in 1989 and have become quite the attraction. It's always fun to watch them bark, lounge around and play with each other.

- Cable car

Let's talk about one of the most iconic things to do in San Francisco - riding a cable car. Not only is it a must-do activity, but it's also a super convenient way to get to Fisherman's Wharf. From Union Square, you can hop on either the Powell-Hyde line or the Powell-Mason line, both of which will take you directly to the Wharf.

If you take the Powell-Hyde line, you'll be dropped off near Ghirardelli Square at Hyde and Beach Street, while the

Powell-Mason line will leave you a few blocks away at Taylor and Bay Street, right in the middle of the Wharf area. Make sure to ride all the way to the end of the line for the full experience.

If you take the Powell-Hyde line, make a quick stop at Lombard Street to check out the world's curviest street before heading down the remaining three steep blocks. It's a fun and quirky experience you won't want to miss!

Our recommendation is to ride one of the cable car lines down to Fisherman's Wharf and the other one back up. This way, you'll get to experience the best of both worlds! Just a heads up, cable car tickets can be pricey, so if you're planning to use public transportation more than once, you may want to consider getting a day pass. Another great option is to download the MuniMobile App, which lets you purchase tickets for cable cars, street cars, and other Muni transportation using your credit card.

- Magowan's Infinite Mirror Maze

Experience a mind-bending adventure in the heart of Pier 39 at Magowan's Infinite Mirror Maze! It's a surreal and immersive journey through a labyrinth of mirrors, lights, and illusions that will challenge your senses in the most fun way possible.

The first thing you'll notice is the infinite reflection of yourself and the people around you, stretching in every direction. It's a mesmerizing sight that immediately sets the tone for the adventure ahead. Once you enter the maze, it's up to you to navigate the twists and turns, all while being surrounded by endless reflections of yourself and your friends.

The maze is full of surprises, with dead ends, looping paths, and even a kaleidoscope-like room that will make you feel like you're floating in space. As you make your way through the maze, you'll encounter a variety of interactive features that will keep you on your toes. For example, there are buttons that trigger light shows, spinning mirrors that distort your reflection, and even secret passages that will lead you to unexpected destinations.

But be warned: the maze is not for the faint of heart. It can be disorienting and challenging, but that's all part of the fun.

Magowan's Infinite Mirror Maze is a thrilling adventure that will make you feel like you're in a different dimension, and you won't want to leave!

- Boat Tour

Take a boat tour of the bay. Grab your sea legs and hop aboard one of the many boat tours available. Trust us, the views are jaw-dropping - think Golden Gate Bridge, Alcatraz Island, and the city skyline. It's like seeing the city in a whole new light! Don't miss out on this awesome adventure. Why not pack a picnic, snap some pics, and make some unforgettable memories on the water? Anchors away!

- Aquarium of the Bay

Dive into the deep blue sea and make a splash at the Aquarium of the Bay! This awesome spot is home to a whopping 30,000 marine animals, from playful penguins to majestic sharks and everything in between. Talk about an aquatic adventure! Not only is it super fun, but you'll also get to learn about the incredible diversity of life that calls the bay home. Want to make the most of your visit? Check out the feeding times and catch your favorite creatures in action, or even get up close and personal with a touch tank experience. Grab your buddies and go make some fishy friends today!

- Shopping

If you are a shopaholic, it's time to hit up Fisherman's Wharf and get your retail therapy fix! From cute souvenirs to trendy threads, the Wharf has got you covered with its awesome array of shops. Trust us, you'll be spoilt for choice. Whether you're hunting for a unique gift or a killer outfit, you're bound to find something that catches your eye.

- Food

Satisfy your taste buds at Fisherman's Wharf - a seafood lover's paradise! From succulent crab and lobster to creamy chowder and crispy fish and chips, the options are endless at the many restaurants lining the Wharf. It's like a seafood extravaganza! Want to mix things up? Try a seafood platter for the ultimate tasting experience. And don't forget to wash it all down with a refreshing drink, like a crisp beer or a fruity cocktail. Want to enjoy your meal with a view? Check out one of the waterfront eateries and take in the gorgeous scenery.

- Ghirardelli Square

Take a sweet stroll down memory lane at Ghirardelli Square. This amazing waterfront complex is a chocoholic's dream, with shops, restaurants, and even a chocolate factory - yum! It's the perfect place to satisfy your sweet tooth while taking in the picturesque views. Trust us, the photo ops are endless! Want to get your shop on? Check out the unique boutiques and souvenir shops, or grab a bite to eat at one of the many delicious restaurants. And don't forget to indulge in some chocolatey goodness - we recommend a hot fudge sundae or a box of assorted chocolates. So, lace up those walking shoes and let's go explore Ghirardelli Square, where every step is a treat!

- Musee Mechanique

Level up your fun meter and journey back in time at the Musee Mechanique. This epic museum is a treasure trove of vintage arcade games and mechanical amusements that are sure to bring out your inner child. It's like stepping into a time machine! From classic pinball machines to quirky fortune tellers, there's something for everyone to enjoy. Plus, the museum's location on Fisherman's Wharf makes it the perfect pit stop during your San Fran adventure. Want to really get into the retro spirit? Dress up in your best vintage threads and take some old-school photos in the photo booth. And who knows, you might just discover a new favorite game.

- See a show

Looking for some epic entertainment to spice up your day? Fisherman's Wharf is home to a variety of shows and performances, from mind-blowing magic shows to hilarious comedy acts and rockin' live music performances. It's like a mini Vegas on the waterfront! Want to take it up a notch? Check out one of the dinner shows for a full night of fun and food. And the best part? You can enjoy the entertainment while taking in the stunning views of the bay. Talk about a win-win situation.

- Cartoon museum

For cartoon lovers, geek out at the Cartoon Art Museum - a mecca for all things cartooning! This incredible museum is jam-packed with a collection of cartoons from all around the globe, showcasing the best of the best in the world of animation. From beloved classics to cutting-edge contemporary works, it's a cartoon wonderland! Want to learn more about the history of cartooning? The museum also features awesome exhibits that dive deep into the fascinating past of this art form. Plus, the friendly and knowledgeable staff are always happy to chat and answer any questions you might have.

- Madame Tussauds

Get star-struck at Madame Tussauds San Francisco - the ultimate wax museum experience. Step into a world of glitz and glamor as you rub shoulders with life-size wax figures of your favorite celebs, historical icons, and other legendary figures. It's like being on the set of your favorite movie! Want to take your experience up a notch? Strike a pose with your favorite wax figure and snap a selfie for the 'gram - your friends won't believe their eyes! Plus, with the museum's prime location in the heart of Fisherman's Wharf, it's the perfect pit stop during your San Fran adventure.

- Ripley's Believe It or Not!

Go get amazed at Ripley's Believe It or Not! - the ultimate museum of the weird and wacky! From bizarre artifacts to strange oddities and everything in between, this place is a treasure trove of mind-bending curiosities from around the world. It's like stepping into a world of wonder and imagination! Want to learn more about the stories behind these unusual objects? The friendly and knowledgeable staff are always on hand to share fascinating facts and tidbits that will blow your mind. Plus, with interactive exhibits and games, you can get in on the fun and become a part of the weird and wonderful world of Ripley's!

- SS Jeremiah O'Brien

Set sail on a voyage through time on the SS Jeremiah O'Brien - a fully restored cargo ship from the World War II era. Step back in time and experience what life was like aboard a historic Liberty Ship, complete with all the sights, sounds, and smells of the high seas! Want to learn more about the role that these ships played in the war effort? The knowledgeable crew and volunteers are always on hand to share fascinating stories and insights into the ship's rich history. Plus, with plenty of interactive exhibits and activities, you can get a hands-on experience of life on board a real WWII-era ship.

- USS Pampanito Museum and Memorial

Dive into the fascinating world of submarines at the **USS Pampanito Museum and Memorial** - a fully restored WWII-era submarine turned museum. The USS Pampanito is housed in the Maritime National Historical Park. Take a deep dive into the history and technology behind this amazing vessel, and learn about the brave men who sailed aboard it. From torpedo tubes to sonar equipment, you'll get an up-close look at all the incredible machinery that made these submarines such a vital part of the war effort. Want to experience what life was like aboard a real submarine? Climb aboard and explore the narrow passageways, cramped crew quarters, and top-secret control rooms for yourself! With plenty of exhibits and artifacts to explore, you'll come away with a newfound appreciation for the incredible courage and skill of the submariners who risked everything to keep our country safe. So, come aboard the USS Pampanito and let your curiosity set sail - it's an adventure you won't forget!

- Truhlsen-Marmor Museum of the Eye

Explore the Truhlsen-Marmor Museum of the Eye - a museum dedicated to the fascinating world of vision and sight. From the intricate structure of the human eye to the latest advances in vision science, this museum has it all. Discover the history of eyeglasses and see how they've evolved over time, from ancient times to modern fashion statements. Immerse yourself in the world of color vision and see how our eyes perceive the rainbow of colors that surround us every day. You'll be amazed at the intricate detail and complexity of the human eye, and the incredible ways in which it processes the world around us. And with interactive exhibits and hands-on displays, you'll get a chance to experience the science of vision firsthand. So, grab your friends and family and come see what the Truhlsen-Marmor Museum of the Eye has in store for you - it's a sight to see!

- The Cannery Gallery at the Academy of Art University.

Don't miss out on The Cannery Gallery at the Academy of Art University. This hidden gem is nestled in the historic Ghirardelli Cannery and is home to some of the most thought-provoking contemporary art exhibits around. With rotating exhibits that showcase a variety of artists and art styles, there's always something new and exciting to see. This is a great place to take  a break from the hustle and bustle of Fisherman's Wharf and step into this tranquil space to immerse yourself in the world of art.

- Visit the Exploratorium

This museum is filled with interactive exhibits that allow you to explore science, art, and human perception. You can get hands-on and experiment with different concepts to deepen your understanding of the world around us. It's a perfect place for curious minds of all ages to have fun and learn something new.

- Chinese American community

Learn more about the Chinese American community at the Chinese Historical Society of America Museum. This museum showcases the history and culture of Chinese Americans through various exhibits. You can learn about the experiences of Chinese immigrants in the US and the significant contributions of Chinese Americans to American society. It's a great place to broaden your knowledge and appreciation of different cultures.

- Don't miss out on having fun at the Escapology Escape Rooms.

Go skydiving, bungee jumping, ziplining, white water rafting, scuba diving, windsurfing, kitesurfing, or sailing. There are various companies offering lessons for these activities at Fisherman's Wharf.

Take a ride on the **SkyRide**. This aerial gondola offers stunning views of the bay and the city skyline. It's a great way to get your heart racing and see the city from a different perspective.

Get your climb on! The San Francisco Bay Area is home to several rock climbing gyms that offer a thrilling and challenging workout. Scale the walls and feel the rush of accomplishment. It's a great way to stay in shape and test your limits.

## Golden Gate Park

Golden Gate Park - the crown jewel of San Francisco! This amazing park spans over 1,000 acres and was established way back in 1870. It's home to many famous attractions like the Japanese Tea Garden, the California Academy of Sciences, and the de Young Museum.

But that's not all, there are also tons of other fun things to do in the park like picnicking, hiking, biking, and even paddle boating on Stow Lake. You can also check out the gorgeous gardens, visit the bison paddock, or just relax and soak up the sun.

Just so you know, Golden Gate Park is NOT located near the Golden Gate Bridge. But don't worry, there is a Golden Gate Bridge park as well, just in case you want to check it out.

Golden Gate Park is massive, like over 1,000 acres huge, and it's over 3 miles long! The park is so wooded that some parts are completely cut off from the sound of traffic. So, unless you're up for spending all day walking, I suggest getting a car or a bike so you can explore the park at your own leisurely pace.

- California Academy of Sciences.

Get ready for an adventure at the California Academy of Sciences. This museum is a treasure trove of natural wonders, from giant dinosaurs to colorful fish and exotic plants. Don't miss the chance to see the stars at the planetarium or explore the mysteries of the rainforest. Plus, the aquarium is a great way to get up close and personal with marine life. It's a perfect destination for science enthusiasts and families alike.

Step into the Osher Rainforest at the California Academy of Sciences for an immersive experience like no other! This indoor rainforest is a replica of the Amazon and is home to a diverse array of plants and animals, including birds, butterflies, and reptiles. It's a fantastic opportunity to learn about the importance of rainforests and how we can protect them. Plus, you can see some of the most fascinating creatures up close and personal, making it an interactive and exciting adventure for visitors of all ages.

- de Young Museum

If you're interested in art, you should definitely check out the de Young Museum. This museum showcases American art from the 1600s all the way up to the present day, so there's plenty to see. In addition to the art, they also have an amazing collection of textiles and costumes from around the world. It's a great way to immerse yourself in different cultures and time periods.

- Conservatory of Flowers

This is the ideal spot to unwind and surround yourself with lush greenery. This tropical paradise is a greenhouse that boasts a variety of exotic and breathtakingly beautiful plants from around the world. It's the perfect place to take a break from the hustle and bustle of the city and immerse yourself in the beauty of nature. The conservatory also hosts special events throughout the year, such as flower shows and live music performances, making it a fun and interactive destination for visitors of all ages. So come on down and bask in the warmth and beauty of this hidden gem in the heart of San Francisco.

- Legion of Honor

Have a blast exploring the Legion of Honor. While not located in Golden Gate Park, Legion of Honor is located in Lincoln

Park which is just a 5-minute drive away. This art museum is a treasure trove of European masterpieces, spanning over 6 centuries from the 14th to the 20th. You'll find stunning paintings, sculptures, and decorative arts that will leave you in awe. And that's not all - the museum also features a collection of ancient Greek and Roman art that will transport you back in time.

- San Francisco Botanical Garden

Explore the San Francisco Botanical Garden, a lush garden that showcases an impressive collection of flora from around the globe. Take a stroll among the towering trees, vibrant flowers, and exotic plants, and let the natural beauty of the garden soothe your soul. The garden also offers a range of educational programs and events for all ages, including guided tours, workshops, and concerts.

- The Walt Disney Family Museum

Step into the world of Walt Disney at The Walt Disney Family Museum. This museum is dedicated to the life and legacy of the famous animator, with exhibits covering his early years, career highlights, and influence on popular culture. Learn all about the creation of beloved characters like Mickey Mouse and explore the magic behind classic Disney films.

- Japanese Tea Garden

Head to the peaceful and serene Japanese Tea Garden nestled in Golden Gate Park. This enchanting garden is a perfect place to escape the hustle and bustle of the city and unwind in the tranquil beauty of Japan. Take a stroll through the garden's winding paths and discover its many hidden gems, including charming bridges, pagodas, and koi ponds. Enjoy a cup of traditional Japanese tea and indulge in delicious Japanese snacks in the Tea House, surrounded by breathtaking views of the garden.

Make sure to visit the authentic Japanese pagoda, one of the oldest structures in the garden, and take a photo with the iconic **Red Torii Gate**. And don't forget to admire the colorful blooms of cherry blossom and azaleas, which are particularly stunning in the spring.

- Bison paddock

Check out the Bison paddock. It's one of the coolest and most hidden attractions in the park. The paddock has been around since 1890 and has been home to American Bison ever since. It's like a time capsule of the wild west!

If you're planning to drive, I recommend parking on John F Kennedy Drive near the paddock. The bison are known to move around the park, but they usually hang out near the barn. Don't be surprised if you have to circle around a bit to get a better view of them. But trust me, it's totally worth it!

- Dutch Windmills

Want to experience a unique and peaceful atmosphere in Golden Gate Park? Look no further than the two Dutch Windmills on the park's west end. These windmills have an amazing history - they used to pump a whopping 1.5 million gallons of water a day to help develop the park! While they may not be pumping anymore, they are surrounded by the beautiful Queen Wilhelmina Tulip Gardens. When spring rolls around, these gardens become a rainbow of colors and it's a sight to behold. Plus, the windmills are just a few blocks away from Ocean Beach, making it the perfect spot to catch the sunset after taking in the view.

Pro tip: plan to visit during Golden Hour for the ultimate experience.

- Stow Lake

Soak in the magic of Stow Lake, a charming body of water nestled in the heart of Golden Gate Park. Home to a delightful variety of birds and turtles, this tranquil lake is the perfect place to unwind and soak in the peaceful atmosphere. Keep an eye out for **Strawberry Hill**, a majestic hill situated in the middle of the lake, and climb to the top for a breathtaking view of the Golden Gate Bridge on a clear day. Stow Lake is full of hidden treasures waiting to be discovered. Check out the Stow Lake Boat House where you can rent paddle boats for a fun and adventurous day on the water. And don't miss the chance to see the beautiful waterfall and Chinese Pavilion, perfect for taking stunning photos and immersing yourself in the park's beauty.

- Shakespeare Garden

For a charming and intimate picnic spot in Golden Gate Park, make sure to visit the Shakespeare Garden. This garden is brimming with plants that were frequently mentioned in Shakespeare's literary works, making it a perfect destination for bookworms. The best part? Despite its location next to the popular California Academy of Sciences, the garden is often overlooked by visitors, so it's an ideal spot for a peaceful and quiet picnic.

- James Turrell Sky Space

Check out The James Turrell Sky Space. It's this awesome spot tucked away behind the de Young Museum that's open 24/7. The coolest part about it is that every visit is unique because the way the space looks changes depending on the time of day and the season. You could visit at noon in April and then again at sunset in September and have totally different experiences. It's also a great spot for Instagram photos, so be sure to bring your camera and snap some pics.

- Beach Chalet Brewery and Restaurant

After a long day of exploring the wonders of Golden Gate Park, there's no better way to unwind than by grabbing a beer and enjoying the beautiful sunset over the ocean at the Beach Chalet. This cozy spot offers a great selection of beers and tasty pub grub. Plus, the ocean view is unbeatable! So kick back, relax, and soak up the stunning scenery as the sun goes down. It's the perfect way to end a perfect day in Golden Gate Park.

## Chinatown

Chinatown is one of the most popular tourist destinations in San Francisco. It is the oldest and one of the largest Chinatowns in the United States. It was established in 1848, during the California Gold Rush, when many Chinese immigrants came to the city in search of work. Today, Chinatown is a bustling neighborhood with a unique mix of traditional Chinese culture and modern-day amenities.

Two of the main streets here are Grant Avenue and Stockton Street. Grant Avenue is the place to go for all the touristy stuff, with tons of shops and restaurants to choose from. You've gotta check out Sing Chong & Sing Fat, a Chinese department store with all kinds of cool stuff; Good Mong Kok Bakery, a bakery that makes the best dim sum; and Jade Emperor's Palace, a Chinese restaurant that's been around for over a century.

Now, if you want a taste of traditional China, head over to Stockton Street. This street is all about fresh produce, herbal remedies, and authentic Chinese cuisine. Stop by Wing Lee Produce Market or Hong Kong Supermarket for some amazing fresh fruits and veggies. And for all your herbal needs, check out Good Luck Herb Company or New May Wah.

When it comes to food, you won't be disappointed on Stockton Street either. Dragon Beaux is a Cantonese restaurant famous for its delicious seafood, Good Luck Dim Sum has been dishing up amazing dim sum for over 30 years, and Shanghai Dumpling King is a Shanghainese restaurant that's known for its scrumptious dumplings.

**Getting There**: The best way to get to Chinatown is by public transportation. You can take the Muni Bus lines 30, 45, or 1 to get there. You can also take the Cable Car lines Powell-Hyde or Powell-Mason, which both have stops in Chinatown.

## Chinatown Bucket List

- Dragon Gate

The awesome entrance to Chinatown. When you're looking to step into another world, head straight for the Dragon Gate on Grant Avenue. You can't miss it - the stunning archway with intricate designs is a perfect photo op for you and your crew. It's the perfect way to start your adventure into the sights, sounds and smells of one of the most exciting neighborhoods in San Francisco.

- Golden Gate Fortune Cookie Factory

Looking for a sweet treat and a unique experience in Chinatown? Look no further than the Golden Gate Fortune Cookie Factory in Ross Alley. Watch as they make fortune cookies fresh right in front of you, and even get a chance to sample some of the delicious cookies straight out of the oven. It's a great spot to pick up a fun and tasty souvenir for yourself or a friend.

- Waverly Place

Welcome to Waverly Place, the heart and soul of San Francisco's Chinatown! Here are some super fun and exciting things to add to your itinerary:

☐ Visit the Tin How Temple

Step into a time machine and get lost in the culture of the oldest Taoist temple in the United States. The detailed architecture is just breathtaking, and it's a perfect place to chill out and catch your breath.

☐ Sample some authentic Chinese cuisine

Waverly Place is home to some of the best Chinese restaurants in San Francisco! Whether you're craving some dumplings or noodles, you're sure to find something that will tantalize your taste buds.

☐ Join a walking tour

Explore Chinatown's history and culture by joining a guided tour. You'll discover hidden gems and have the opportunity to see the neighborhood in a whole new light.

☐ Shop till you drop:

Waverly Place has shops selling traditional Chinese clothing, souvenirs, and other trinkets. Wander through the shops and find that perfect souvenir to take home.

☐ Experience the nightlife

Waverly Place has an exciting nightlife with something for everyone. Whether you want to dance the night away or have a chill night out with friends, you'll find a spot that's perfect for you.

- Portsmouth Square

See Portsmouth Square, the heart of Chinatown. This bustling plaza is a must-visit spot for people-watching and immersing yourself in the vibrant energy of the neighborhood. You'll see locals playing games like mahjong and Chinese chess, street performers showcasing their talents, and food vendors selling tasty treats. Be sure to take in the sights and sounds around you, and don't forget to snap some photos of this historic spot.

- Chinese Historical Society of America Museum

Visit the Chinese Historical Society of America Museum. This museum is dedicated to preserving and sharing the history and culture of Chinese Americans. It's a great place to learn more about the history of Chinatown and the Chinese American community.

- Grant Avenue

Explore Grant Avenue. This is the main street in Chinatown and it's filled with shops, restaurants, and other attractions. Be sure to check out the many street vendors selling everything from souvenirs to fresh produce. When exploring Grant Avenue, be sure to visit the iconic Old St. Mary Cathedral. This stunning church is a historic landmark and boasts beautiful architecture that is sure to impress.

- Clock tower

Don't forget to stop by the clock tower, which is another must-see attraction on Grant Avenue. Take a selfie with the tower and capture the essence of this vibrant neighborhood.

As you continue your journey down Grant Avenue, you'll come across many other notable landmarks. The Bank of America Building is a towering structure that dominates the skyline, and its unique design is a sight to behold.

Another famous spot is the Golden Gate Bakery, which is famous for its egg custard tarts. You'll definitely want to stop here and indulge in this delicious treat!

Grant Avenue is also home to many shops selling everything from traditional Chinese clothing to modern-day souvenirs. So, if you're looking for some retail therapy, be sure to take a stroll down this bustling street.

## Union Square

Union Square is one of the city's most popular tourist destinations, and for good reason.

Union Square has a fascinating history. It was named after a series of pro-Union rallies that were held there during the Civil War. Today, it's a bustling square that is surrounded by some of the city's best shopping, dining, and entertainment options.

**Getting to Union Square**

- BART (Bay Area Rapid Transit): If you're coming from outside San Francisco, BART is a great option. Take BART to the Powell Street station, and you'll be just a few blocks away from Union Square.

- Muni: San Francisco's municipal transit system, Muni, offers a number of bus and train lines that stop near Union Square. The 2-Clement, 3-Jackson, 38-Geary, and 45-Union/Stockton buses all stop right at or near Union Square.

- Cable car: Taking a cable car to Union Square is a classic San Francisco experience. The Powell-Hyde and Powell-Mason lines both stop near Union Square.

- Shopping

Get ready to shop until you drop at Union Square, the ultimate shopping destination in San Francisco! This area boasts an incredible selection of shops, from the luxury department stores of Neiman Marcus and Saks Fifth Avenue to designer boutiques such as Chanel and Gucci. Whether you're looking for a statement piece or a bargain buy, Union Square has got you covered.

- Food

Looking for a juicy steak? Head over to Morton's The Steakhouse for a mouthwatering meal. If you're in the mood for something sweet, stop by The Cheesecake Factory for a slice of their famous cheesecake. For a fancy dining experience, the Rotunda at Neiman Marcus offers a beautiful setting with stunning views of the city. Other great options include E&O Kitchen and Bar for delicious Asian fusion cuisine and Tadich Grill for fresh seafood.

- Entertainment

Looking for some entertainment in the city? Then you will be sure to find some at Union Square. With the **American Conservatory Theater** right in the heart of the area, you can enjoy a night out on the town watching a fantastic show. If movies are more your thing, check out the **Westfield San Francisco Centre**, which has a great movie theater. Don't forget to grab some popcorn and candy to complete the experience.

- Relaxation

Looking for a relaxing way to spend your day? Then grab a seat in Union Square and enjoy the ultimate people-watching experience. With a wide selection of nearby cafes and eateries, you can sit back with a cup of coffee or a snack, and simply observe the bustling city life around you. It's the perfect spot for a laid-back afternoon or a leisurely break from shopping or sightseeing.

# Haight-Ashbury

Haight-Ashbury is a neighborhood in San Francisco that's famous for its role in the counterculture movement of the

1960s. It's a vibrant and colorful area that's worth a visit, whether you're a hippie at heart or just looking for a unique experience.

Haight Street

Let's talk about the groovy vibes of Haight-Ashbury. Back in the '60s, this neighborhood was the place to be for anyone who wanted to live life differently. It was packed with creative folks, activists, and musicians who believed in love, peace, and freedom. The psychedelic rock scene was also huge here, with epic bands like the Grateful Dead and Jefferson Airplane performing at local venues. Today, Haight-Ashbury is still just as cool and draws in lots of visitors who want to experience its free-spirited, bohemian atmosphere.

Back in the late 1800s, Haight-Ashbury was just a quiet neighborhood on the outskirts of San Francisco. It was a peaceful spot where people could escape the hustle and bustle of the city. Fast forward to the 1950s and 60s, and Haight-Ashbury had become the place to be for the counterculture movement. This neighborhood was filled with artists, musicians, and activists who promoted peace, love, and a new way of life. The Summer of Love in 1967 put this district on the map, with people flocking from all over the country to experience the free-spirited culture. It was the birthplace of iconic bands like the Grateful Dead, Janis Joplin, and Jefferson Airplane, who performed free concerts in nearby Golden Gate Park.

Haight-Ashbury is a funky and vibrant neighborhood with tons of vintage shops, record stores, and fun cafes. The best way to experience it all is by taking a leisurely stroll, taking in the colorful street art and charming Victorian houses. There are a few places you absolutely can't miss, like the **Red Victorian Bed & Breakfast**, a former hotspot for counterculture folks, and the famous Haight-Ashbury intersection, which boasts a bright and lively mural that will leave you feeling inspired.

If you're a vintage fashion lover, you definitely won't want to miss out on Haight-Ashbury. This funky neighborhood is a treasure trove of vintage shops, like Wasteland and Held Over, where you can score some groovy finds from the 60s and 70s or 90s grunge gear. Music aficionados can check out Amoeba Music, a record store with a massive collection of vinyl and CDs. Whether you're searching for some retro threads or just browsing for fun, Haight-Ashbury won't disappoint!

Haight-Ashbury is not just a place for vintage fashion and record stores, but also a destination for foodies! Whether you're a vegan or not, you'll find some tasty plant-based meals at the neighborhood's popular restaurants like Cha-Ya and Shizen. And if you're craving something sweet, head over to The Ice Cream Bar, which has been scooping up delicious handmade ice cream for over 80 years!

**Getting to Haight-Ashbury**

To get to Haight-Ashbury, you can take the Muni bus lines 6, 7, or 33 which also stop on Haight Street. If you're coming from downtown, take the 6 or 7 from Market Street. The neighborhood is also accessible via the N-Judah streetcar, which runs along Haight Street. If you're driving, there are a few public parking lots in the area, but street parking can be challenging to find.

If you're coming from other parts of the city, you can use the Trip Planner feature on the SFMTA website to find the best route for you.

## Haight-Ashbury Bucket List

- Amoeba Music

If you're a music lover, don't miss a trip to Amoeba Music in Haight-Ashbury, San Francisco. It's the biggest indie music store on the planet! They have a mind-boggling selection of records, CDs, and movies. Plus, they put on free shows every month at their Haight Street location. You never know who you might see performing, so drop in and check out their schedule ahead of time.

- Buena Vista Park

Ready for a bit of exercise with a stunning payoff? Head over to Buena Vista Park, located on the eastern side of

Haight-Ashbury's shopping district. This park is packed with lush trees and steep paths that lead to some of the best views of San Francisco and the Bay. To get there, start at the corner of Haight Street and Buena Vista Avenue, and climb the stairs to the top. The trail will wind its way up, but trust me, it's worth it. It typically takes around 30 to 40 minutes to make it to the top, but once you do, you'll be rewarded with breathtaking views that will make you glad you took the trek.

- Murals

Check out the rad murals in Haight-Ashbury! This neighborhood is filled with vibrant and colorful street art, and it's a must-see for any art lover. You'll find awesome murals all over Haight Street and other spots in the district. So take a stroll and keep your eyes peeled for some real gems. One of the coolest murals features Jimi Hendrix, Janis Joplin, and Jerry Garcia – all legendary musicians who lived in Haight-Ashbury during the Summer of Love. You can find this epic mural on Cole Street at Haight – it's totally Instagram-worthy.

- Haunted Haight Tour

If you're up for a spooky adventure, then take the Haunted Haight tour. You'll get to explore the neighborhood at night and visit some of its most haunted spots. But if you're looking for something a little more lighthearted, try the **Hippie Culture City Exploration Game Tour**. It's a self-guided tour that takes you through the vibrant district and lets you go at your own pace. Plus, it's like a game, so it's super fun! The tour takes about 1.5 to 2 hours to complete, but you can take breaks and stop whenever you want.

- Free Walking Tour

Get to know the Haight-Ashbury neighborhood with a free walking tour from the public library. These tours cover everything from the history of the area to specific topics of interest. The Haight tour delves into the original roots of the neighborhood, and the best part is that it's completely free! No need to sign up ahead of time, just show up and start walking. The only downside is that sometimes the groups can get pretty big, making it a little hard to hear the guide.

Hop on a bus and head over to the Lower Haight, a super cool spot that's tucked away and perfect for a chill time. You'll get to chow down like a true local.

## Lombard Street

Lombard Street is nestled in the cool Russian Hill neighborhood of San Francisco, California. It was born back in 1862 and got its name from the twisty roads of Italy's Lombard region. But hold on, it wasn't famous for being a zigzag wonder just yet!

Back in the late 19th century, San Francisco faced a tricky challenge with its hilly landscape. The steep slopes of Russian Hill made it tough for folks to get around, whether they were in cars or on foot. But fear not! Engineer J.R. Thompson had a genius idea up his sleeve. He suggested creating a curvy road with switchbacks to make it easier to tackle those slopes.

Fast forward to 1922, and voila! A stretch of Lombard Street between Hyde and Leavenworth Streets transformed into a mesmerizing maze of eight hairpin turns. Landscape architect

Carl Henry designed these sharp curves that not only looked amazing but also made it practical to conquer the hill's steepness. And just like that, Lombard Street became an instant hit, attracting locals and tourists alike!

As time went by, Lombard Street's fame skyrocketed. It became a superstar, featuring in films, postcards, and travel guides, cementing its status as an iconic symbol of San Francisco. The street's unique allure lured hordes of visitors, and with that came a traffic challenge for the nearby residents.

So, what did they do? In the groovy 1960s, Lombard Street had a makeover party! It got a fresh new pavement, and those sharp curves got even tighter. Now, if you take a stroll or drive along Lombard Street, you'll be greeted by a delightful brick-paved road, meticulously manicured gardens, and a colorful bouquet of flowers lining the route.

Today, Lombard Street is the place to be! It's a magnet for tourists, drawing millions of excited visitors each year. People flock here to soak up the stunning views of San Francisco's sparkling skyline, the majestic Bay, and the iconic Golden Gate Bridge. It's like stepping into a postcard and living the San Francisco dream!

Lombard Street's history is pretty darn impressive, and its unique design continues to capture the hearts of people from all over the world. It's a shining example of San Francisco's creativity and problem-solving skills, triumphing over those challenging hills. So, come on over and experience the wonder of Lombard Street for yourself. Trust me, it's a must-see destination that'll leave you in awe.

## Lombard Street Bucket List

Hop in your car and drive up to the tippity-top of Crooked Street, where Lombard Street meets Hyde. Get ready for a thrilling adventure as you tackle not one, not two, but eight hairpin turns all the way down Lombard Street. It's like being on a roller coaster, but with your own wheels!

Don't have a car? No worries! Hop on the Powell-Hyde Cable Car and let it whisk you up to the summit of Lombard Street.

You'll enjoy a scenic ride and get a front-row seat to the excitement.

Feeling more active? Lace up your walking shoes and take on the challenge of the 250 stairs that flank Lombard Street. Going downhill is a breeze, but beware, the climb back up can be a bit tough. But hey, the stunning views across North Beach and Telegraph Hill are totally worth it!

As you make your way down Lombard Street, keep your eyes peeled for famous landmarks. Spot the majestic twin towers of Saints Peter and Paul Church, catch a glimpse of the iconic Oakland Bay Bridge, and marvel at the beauty of Coit Tower. It's like playing a game of "I Spy" with San Francisco's most iconic sights.

And here's a fun fact for you: Lombard Street used to be paved with cobblestones and had a crazy gradient of 27%, making it quite the challenge for cars to navigate safely. But in 1922, the crooked street design was introduced, reducing the gradient to a still-impressive 16%. So, go ahead and measure that slope while you're there!

Don't forget to admire the gorgeous garden beds that line Lombard Street. If you visit in the spring, you'll be treated to a riot of color as the magnificent hydrangeas bloom. It's like walking through a floral wonderland!

Of course, no visit to Lombard Street is complete without snapping a photo at the base. That's where the action is! Join the crowd and watch in awe as cars expertly maneuver those eight hairpin turns. It's a sight you won't want to miss.

Oh, and here's a bonus tip for you adventurous explorers: if you want to check out San Francisco's real most crooked street without the tourist crowds, head over to Vermont Street on Potrero Hill, between 20th and 22nd. It may not be as pretty as Lombard Street, but it's still delightfully crooked and largely undiscovered by tourists. It's like finding a hidden gem!

## Vermont Street

While it may not have the same superstar status as Lombard Street, this crooked gem in San Francisco's Potrero Hill neighborhood has its own story to tell.

Back in the late 19th century, as part of the city's urban development, Vermont Street came to life. It was named after the beautiful state of Vermont, giving a nod to its eastern counterpart. Over time, houses popped up along the street, creating a charming residential area.

Unlike Lombard Street, Vermont Street didn't start out intentionally crooked. Nope, its twists and turns were a gift from Mother Nature herself, thanks to San Francisco's hilly landscape. The steep slopes and curves made it quite the adventure for anyone trying to get around, whether on foot or in a vehicle.

Now, here's the exciting part: Vermont Street remained somewhat of a hidden secret for a while, largely unknown to tourists. But hey, that didn't stop it from oozing its own unique charm! Locals appreciated its off-the-radar allure and cherished its one-of-a-kind character.

But hold on, things have been changing in recent years! Vermont Street has been getting some well-deserved recognition as a quirky attraction. Its snaking layout, with sharp turns and bends, has caught the eye of curious visitors looking for an alternative crooked street experience. It's like finding a hidden treasure right in the heart of San Francisco!

Today, Vermont Street offers an adventure off the beaten path. It's the perfect spot for those who want to explore the crooked streets beyond Lombard Street. Get ready to soak in the picturesque views and follow the winding path as you discover this hidden gem. It's a charming and unique experience that'll make you fall in love with San Francisco all over again.

Sure, Vermont Street may not have the same fame or bustling crowds as Lombard Street, but it has its own special place in the city's history. It adds to the vibrant tapestry of San

Francisco's streetscape, showcasing the city's diversity and hidden treasures.

So, if you're up for a different kind of crooked adventure in San Francisco, make sure to put Vermont Street on your list. It's just waiting to be explored, and trust me, you won't be disappointed. Get ready for a fun-filled and charming experience like no other.

# CHAPTER FOUR

## Neighborhoods and Districts

### Castro

Located in the lively Eureka Valley district, Castro is famous for its vibrant LGBTQ+ community. It's no wonder it holds a special place in the history of gay neighborhoods in the United States and has been a driving force in the LGBTQ+ rights movement.

The Castro neighborhood is an awesome and lively place to visit. It's known as the hub of the city's LGBTQ+ community and has a rich history of activism and diversity. The neighborhood is home to many cool businesses, shops, restaurants, and nightlife options that cater to the LGBTQ+ community, but it's welcoming to everyone, no matter what background you come from.

This neighborhood is bursting with life and color, and it's easy to spot thanks to all the rainbow flags waving proudly from the flagpoles, storefronts, and crosswalks. You've arrived at the city's famous gay district and one of the most well-known LGBTQ+ areas in the world.

At the Castro, you'll be surrounded by vibrant rainbow flags in every direction you turn - it's like a rainbow exploded in the best way possible!

The Castro is named after José Castro, who was a leader during California's early history. The neighborhood has changed a lot over time, but it's been a cornerstone of the LGBTQ+ community since the 60s and 70s. It was also a center of activism during the AIDS epidemic in the 80s and 90s, and some amazing LGBTQ+ figures and organizations emerged from the area.

So, if you're looking for a fun and colorful atmosphere, the Castro is the place to be! You can explore its many shops and eateries, take in a show at the historic Castro Theatre, and learn all about its rich history and contributions to LGBTQ+ rights and culture at the GLBT History Museum. Plus, if you time your visit right, you might catch some of the neighborhood's awesome annual events, like the Castro Street Fair or the San Francisco Pride Parade.

Getting to the Castro is a breeze thanks to the convenient public transportation options available. Hop on one of the many bus lines or take a ride on the F-Market streetcar line to reach this exciting destination.

Situated between Market Street to the north, 17th Street to the south, Dolores Street to the east, and Clarendon Avenue to the west, the Castro is perfectly positioned for exploration. It's surrounded by other fantastic neighborhoods that are just a short stroll away. Take a leisurely walk to the trendy Mission District, the stylish Hayes Valley, or the elegant Nob Hill, and discover even more of what San Francisco has to offer.

## The Castro Bucket List

- **Rainbow Honor Walk**

Make sure to check out the Rainbow Honor Walk. It's a sidewalk display featuring plaques that honor the people who've fought for the equality and rights of the LGBTQ+ community. You'll learn all about the history of the area and the amazing folks who made it what it is today.

Be sure to hit up the many vintage shops for some unique finds. And when you're ready for a sweet treat, head on over to **Castro Fountain Bakery** for their famous rainbow cake. Trust us, you won't want to miss out on this colorful and delicious dessert! So, let's get shopping and treat ourselves to some yummy sweets - it's the perfect way to round out a day in the Castro District.

- Castro Theater

Make sure to check out the Castro Theater. This beautiful theater was built back in 1922 and was designed by the talented Timothy L Pflueger, who also designed other iconic buildings in California, like the Paramount Theater in Oakland. But the fun doesn't stop there! The Castro hosts a variety of festivals and events throughout the year that celebrate love, diversity, and equality. Join in the festivities at the **Castro Street Fair** or be a part of the spectacular San Francisco Pride Parade, where the neighborhood truly comes alive with joy and pride.

- Castro Street

Stroll down Castro Street, the bustling main thoroughfare, and marvel at the vibrant and eye-catching murals that adorn its walls. And don't forget to stop by Twin Peaks Tavern, a legendary gay bar that has been serving the community for ages.

If you're looking to expand your exploration beyond the Castro District, I've got a suggestion for you. Just a short walk away is the Mission District, and it's definitely worth checking out. This neighborhood is famous for its stunning street art and murals, and it's the perfect place to add to your itinerary after exploring the Castro.

Whether you're a member of the LGBTQ+ community or an ally, Castro welcomes you with open arms. It's a place where diversity is celebrated, and equality is cherished.
I suggest taking a walking tour around the Castro, then making your way over to the Mission District to see some of the amazing artwork that makes this neighborhood so special. It's a perfect combination of exploring two unique areas in San Francisco - so get walking and see what this city has to offer.

## Marina

Back in the day, this area was a tidal marshland called Black Point Cove, until it was filled in with rubble and debris after the 1906 earthquake to create new land.

In 1915, the Palace of Fine Arts was built for the Panama-Pacific Exposition, which celebrated the completion of the Panama Canal and showcased San Francisco's revival after the quake. However, the palace was later neglected and had to be rebuilt in the 1960s.

During World War II, the Marina became a crucial departure point for military personnel and supplies heading to the Pacific Theater. But after the war, many of the buildings were converted into homes and apartments, turning the Marina into a highly sought-after residential area.

Back in the 1989 Loma Prieta earthquake, the Marina was hit hard, with many buildings damaged and streets closed for months during reconstruction.

But today, the Marina is back and better than ever! It's a lively neighborhood known for its gorgeous views of the Golden Gate Bridge, fantastic shopping and dining spots, and lovely parks and iconic landmarks. Even with its tough past, the Marina is still a top spot for both visitors and San Franciscans alike.

Situated along the stunning San Francisco Bay, the Marina offers incredible views that will leave you in awe. Get ready to feast your eyes on the world-famous Golden Gate Bridge and the mysterious Alcatraz Island, all from the comfort of this fantastic neighborhood. As you stroll along the marina, you'll spot boats gracefully docked and people indulging in various water activities, adding an extra touch of charm to the scenery.

Here's a fun fact: the Marina boasts a flat terrain, which sets it apart from the hilly landscape found in many other parts of the city. This makes it a hotspot for walking, jogging, and cycling enthusiasts. Embrace the outdoors and take advantage of the picturesque Marina Green Park, where you can bask in the sun, have a picnic, or engage in some friendly outdoor games.

When it comes to architectural styles, the Marina offers a delightful mix. You'll encounter elegant Victorian and Edwardian homes that exude charm and character, alongside modern condominiums and apartment buildings. This diversity gives the neighborhood a unique flair, making every street a joy to explore. Don't forget to check out the vibrant boutiques, mouthwatering restaurants, cozy cafes, and lively bars that line the lively streets of the Marina.

And let's not forget about the Marina's buzzing nightlife! Make your way to the energetic Chestnut Street, where you'll find a plethora of entertainment options. From trendy bars to exciting nightclubs, there's something for everyone. Dance the night away, sip on delicious cocktails, or simply enjoy a refreshing drink.

Streets in Marina

**Chestnut Street**: Brace yourself for an energy-packed stroll down the heart and soul of the Marina. Chestnut Street is a buzzing hub bursting with life! Explore a diverse array of shops, trendy boutiques, and mouthwatering restaurants and cafes. Whether you're hunting for stylish threads, satisfying your cravings, or simply people-watching over a cup of joe, Chestnut Street has it all.

**Union Street**: Parallel to Chestnut Street, Union Street is another hotspot you won't want to miss. Prepare to be charmed by its enchanting Victorian architecture. This delightful street invites you to discover trendy shops, stylish boutiques, and cozy cafes. Unleash your inner fashionista, find unique local treasures, and treat yourself to tantalizing delights.

**Lombard Street**: Hold on tight as we venture outside the Marina to the world-famous Lombard Street. Known as the "crookedest street in the world," this iconic attraction between Hyde and Leavenworth Streets features eight mind-boggling hairpin turns. Prepare to be amazed and capture unforgettable moments as you witness the essence of San Francisco's unique character.

**Marina Boulevard**: Picture-perfect views await you along Marina Boulevard, running parallel to the bay. Marvel at the breathtaking waterfront and catch a glimpse of the majestic Golden Gate Bridge. This scenic boulevard is a haven for leisurely walks, invigorating jogs, and thrilling bike rides. Immerse yourself in the refreshing sea breeze, soak up the panoramic vistas, and embrace the natural beauty surrounding you.

**Fillmore Street**: Just a hop, skip, and a jump away from the Marina, Fillmore Street beckons with upscale boutiques, art galleries, and charming cafes. As one of the city's premier shopping destinations, Fillmore Street invites fashion enthusiasts and treasure seekers to uncover stylish finds and hidden gems. Keep an eye out for cultural events and festive celebrations that make this street come alive throughout the year.

Cervantes Boulevard: Venture along Cervantes Boulevard, a picturesque stretch bordering the Presidio. Get ready for awe-inspiring views of the bay, the majestic Golden Gate Bridge, and the lush greenery of the Presidio's forests. Whether you prefer a leisurely stroll or a breezy bike ride, this scenic boulevard invites you to bask in tranquility and immerse yourself in nature's splendor.

## Marina Bucket List

- Palace of Fine Arts.

Experience the enchanting beauty of the Palace of Fine Arts in the Marina District. This stunning structure was originally built for the 1915 Panama-Pacific Exposition and has since become a beloved landmark of San Francisco.

- Lagoon

Take a stroll around the peaceful lagoon and marvel at the majestic Greco-Roman architecture, adorned with intricate details and sculptures. It's the perfect place for a romantic walk or a peaceful picnic. Don't forget to snap some photos to capture the ethereal beauty of this iconic San Francisco spot!

- Crissy Field

If you're looking for more to do in the Marina, there's plenty to explore. Head over to Crissy Field for a scenic walk or bike ride, or check out the trendy shops and restaurants along Chestnut Street. And of course, you can't miss out on the stunning views of the Golden Gate Bridge from the Marina Green. So come on down to the Marina and experience the magic for yourself!

- Marina Green

Let's talk about the Marina Green, an awesome park that you can't miss when visiting the Marina district. It used to be an airfield for the U.S. Post Office, but now it's a huge grassy area with breathtaking views of the Bay, the Golden Gate Bridge, and Alcatraz Island. It's perfect for kite flying, soaking up the sun, or playing a game of volleyball.

Marina Green also has some really cool things to check out too! First, there's the Wave Organ, an amazing sculpture made of PVC and concrete organ pipes that creates beautiful sounds using the power of the changing tides. It's an experience you won't forget!

If you're looking to get active, the Marina Green Fitness Court is also a great option. It's a seven-station circuit-training system designed for outdoor workouts. So, you can work up a sweat while taking in the stunning views of the Bay.

If you happen to visit San Francisco during **Fleet Week** in October, don't miss out on the thrilling performances by the Blue Angels flight demo squadron, and the Marina Green is one of the best spots to witness their daredevil stunts firsthand. The Green serves as a perfect vantage point to watch the squadron's incredible maneuvers against the backdrop of the iconic Golden Gate Bridge and Alcatraz Island. Make sure to grab a seat early to secure your spot for the show.

Experience the thrill of "going off the grid" at San Francisco's ultimate food truck gathering! From March to October on Friday evenings, head to the Fort Mason parking lot for a foodie feast like no other. With over 30 food trucks and mobile food stations serving up delicious eats, as well as craft beer, wine, and cocktails to quench your thirst, you won't be disappointed. Groove to live music and DJ beats, hang out in the central beer garden and enjoy stunning bay views at this end-of-week celebration. Don't miss out on the chance to sample some of the most authentic and delicious street food in the country.

Unlike the rest of San Francisco, the Marina District is super flat - great for easygoing cyclists who'd rather soak up the stunning views than work up a sweat tackling the city's steep hills. Along Lombard Street, there are several bike rental spots to choose from, including Parkwide Bike Rentals at Fort

Mason. They not only offer bike rentals but also have guided tours that'll take you over the Golden Gate Bridge to Sausalito, through Golden Gate Park, and even across the city on motor-assisted electric bikes. For even more incredible views of the Golden Gate Bridge heading west, hop on the Bay Trail which connects Fisherman's Wharf to the Presidio's Crissy Field via the Marina.

## North Beach

North Beach's story takes us back to the early days of San Francisco, where it began as a bustling port town during the California Gold Rush. As time went on, it evolved into a vibrant neighborhood that attracted Italian immigrants, leaving an indelible mark on its identity as the hub of Italian culture and cuisine.

Located in the northeastern part of the city, North Beach sits pretty next to the bustling Financial District, with Chinatown, Telegraph Hill, and Fisherman's Wharf as its neighbors. And guess what? Its prime location near the waterfront means you can easily embark on epic adventures to iconic spots like the Golden Gate Bridge and Alcatraz Island.

Streets and Attractions:

Let's hit the streets, starting with the fabulous **Columbus Avenue**! Brace yourself for an explosion of character and charm. It's the main thoroughfare of North Beach, where vibrant Italian cafes, bustling restaurants, and authentic delis await. The enticing aroma of fresh bread and savory sauces will make your taste buds dance with joy!

For a breath of fresh air and some community vibes, head to **Washington Square Park**. This green oasis in the heart of North Beach is the perfect spot to unwind, play, and enjoy local events. Soak in the neighborhood's atmosphere and let the good vibes rejuvenate your spirit.

Just a hop, skip, and a jump away is **Grant Avenue,** the backbone of neighboring Chinatown. This cultural adventure playground will dazzle you with its vibrant streets, Chinese markets, and traditional eateries. Get ready to unleash your senses and dive into an extraordinary culinary journey.

**Getting to North Beach:**

101

**By Bus**: Hop on the 8, 30, or 45 bus lines that serve North Beach. Stay updated on schedules and routes by checking out the San Francisco Municipal Transportation Agency (SFMTA) website.

**By Cable Car**: Feel like a true San Franciscan and ride the Powell-Hyde or Powell-Mason cable car lines. Hop off at the Washington Square stop, and voila! You're ready to explore North Beach on foot.

**By BART:** If you're coming from outside the city, take the BART (Bay Area Rapid Transit) to the Montgomery Street station. From there, it's a short walk or a quick bus ride to North Beach.

**Pro tip**: Double-check transit schedules and plan your trip using reliable sources like the SFMTA website or mobile apps to ensure you have the most up-to-date information.

North Beach Bucket List

- Coit Tower

Reach for the skies at Coit Tower. This iconic landmark offers mind-blowing views of the city that'll take your breath away. Coit tower sits on Telegraph Hill which is a neighborhood overlapping North Beach. Get your camera ready for some epic selfies.

- Food

Mangia, mangia! Explore Italian delights: North Beach is a paradise for foodies, especially if you're craving scrumptious Italian cuisine. Dive into a plate of pasta or savor some delectable pizza at one of the best Italian restaurants in town.

- Nightlife

Get your groove on in North Beach's nightlife: Looking for a good time? North Beach is the place to be! Hop from one cool bar to another, sip on delicious cocktails, and dance the night away to live music. The party never stops in this vibrant neighborhood!

- Beat Museum

Step back in time at the Beat Museum. Immerse yourself in the world of the Beat Generation at this groovy museum.

Discover the lives and works of the rebellious writers and poets who called North Beach home in the 1950s. It's a trip you won't want to miss!

Stroll through Washington Square Park: Lace up your walking shoes and take a leisurely stroll through this popular park. It's the perfect spot to relax, people-watch, and soak up the lively atmosphere that North Beach has to offer. Don't forget to snap some insta-worthy pics!

- Ferry Building Marketplace

Shop 'til you drop at the Ferry Building Marketplace. Get ready for a shopping extravaganza at this bustling marketplace. Explore a variety of shops offering unique treasures and treat yourself to delicious bites from local restaurants. It's a shopper's paradise!

## Mission

Welcome to the Mission, a vibrant neighborhood bursting with history and diversity! It all began with the establishment of Mission San Francisco de Asís (aka Mission Dolores) in 1776, which led to the development of a thriving community.

Throughout the years, waves of immigrants from Ireland, Germany, Italy, and more contributed to the neighborhood's multicultural fabric. In the 20th century, the Mission became a hub for Latinx communities and played a pivotal role in the city's Chicano and LGBTQ+ movements.

Geographically, the Mission is nestled between Potrero Hill and Bernal Heights in the eastern part of San Francisco. It's bordered by Market Street to the north, Cesar Chavez Street to the south, Dolores Street to the east, and Valencia Street to the west. Its central location makes it a breeze to access downtown San Francisco and other nearby areas.

Mission Street is where the action happens, stretching from the Embarcadero to the southern end of the city. Picture a vibrant street lined with diverse shops, tantalizing taquerias, mouthwatering restaurants, and cultural institutions. This bustling thoroughfare truly captures the neighborhood's lively spirit!

Valencia Street is another hot spot in the Mission, known for its hip and eclectic vibe. It's a haven for trendsetters, featuring trendy boutiques, awe-inspiring art galleries, cozy cafes, and happening bars. Prepare for an artsy adventure and soak up the creative energy of this vibrant street.

Now, let's talk about getting to the Mission using public transportation. Here's the scoop:

By BART: BART (Bay Area Rapid Transit) has got you covered! Hop on a BART train and head to the 16th Street Mission Station, located right in the heart of the neighborhood. Once you arrive, you can easily explore the Mission on foot and soak up the lively atmosphere.

By Bus: Several bus lines run through the Mission, providing easy access to different parts of the neighborhood. Look out for the 14-Mission, 49-Van Ness/Mission, and 22-Fillmore bus lines. For accurate and up-to-date bus routes and schedules, check out the San Francisco Municipal Transportation Agency (SFMTA) website.

By Bike: The Mission is a paradise for cyclists! With dedicated bike lanes and bike-sharing programs, you can pedal your way through the neighborhood at your own pace. Soak up the vibrant streets and enjoy the freedom of exploring on two wheels!

## Mission Bucket List

Get ready for a taste bud fiesta at the Mission's incredible array of taquerias, pupuserias, and other Latino restaurants! From mouthwatering tacos to savory pupusas, you'll embark on a culinary adventure that will leave you craving more. Pro tip: Don't forget to try the delicious horchata or refreshing agua fresca to wash it all down!

- Mission Dolores

Step back in time and visit Mission Dolores, the oldest surviving building in San Francisco. Explore its historic walls, stroll through the tranquil gardens, and learn about the mission's fascinating past. It's a must-see for history buffs and a great spot to capture Insta-worthy photos!

- Clarion Alley and Balmy Alley

Get your art appreciation game on and discover the vibrant murals of Clarion Alley and Balmy Alley. These captivating outdoor galleries showcase the creativity and talent of local artists. Each mural tells a story, so take your time, snap some selfies, and immerse yourself in the colorful world of street art.

- Dolores Park

Get your hiking boots on and conquer the summit of Dolores Park for breathtaking views of the city. This elevated oasis offers panoramic vistas that will leave you in awe. Whether you're enjoying a picnic or joining a friendly game of frisbee, Dolores Park is the place to be for stunning sights and outdoor fun.

- Mission-style burrito

Prepare your taste buds for a culinary adventure you won't want to miss in this corner of the city. We're talking about the legendary Mission-style burrito, and trust us, it's no joke. Make sure you work up a good appetite because this burrito is a hearty beast you'll want to conquer.

Picture this: a steamed flour tortilla, so perfectly flexible that it can contain a massive amount of scrumptious ingredients. The result? Pure deliciousness wrapped in a tortilla blanket.

- Urban Putt

Get ready to tee off in a whole new way! If you're up for a round of mini-golf that breaks all the traditional rules, Urban Putt is the place to be. This isn't your grandma's mini-golf—it's a wild combination of mini-golf and crazy art installations that will blow your mind!

Step inside an old Victorian-style home that dates back to 1906, and you'll find yourself immersed in a mini-golf experience like no other. Urban Putt boasts 14 high-tech and totally unconventional holes that will challenge your skills and ignite your imagination. From mind-bending obstacles to quirky designs, each hole is a work of art in itself.

Urban Putt isn't just about golf. It's a complete entertainment destination with a full restaurant and bar. So, before you grab your putter and golf ball, head over to the bar for a refreshing cocktail or your favorite drink. Relax, unwind, and let the good times flow as you prepare to conquer the course.

When it comes to playing golf at Urban Putt, it's a first-come, first-served basis. But don't worry! Even if there's a short wait, the bar will be there to take care of you. Sip on your favorite beverage, chat with your friends, and get into the swing of things.

- Carnaval

Just like Mardi Gras sets New Orleans on fire with its vibrant spirit, Carnaval sets San Francisco ablaze with a similar kind of energy! This incredible celebration pays homage to the rich cultures of Latino, Caribbean, and African communities deeply rooted in The Mission neighborhood. Get ready for two wild days of non-stop fun!

Mark your calendars for the last weekend of May, because that's when the magic happens. Harrison Street between 16th and 24th streets becomes the ultimate hotspot, drawing crowds of enthusiastic revelers. It's a massive celebration of multiculturalism, and you won't want to miss it!

As you wander through the lively streets, you'll encounter a symphony of music and dance that fills the air. From the infectious beats of salsa and reggae to the rhythmic sounds of African drums, every corner becomes a stage for talented performers. And let's not forget about the mouthwatering food! Indulge in a feast for your taste buds, with street tacos and traditional Caribbean delights just waiting to be savored.

But that's not all! The climax of Carnaval is an extraordinary parade that will leave you speechless. Imagine a spectacle of colors and costumes that defy imagination. From extravagant feathers to sparkling sequins, the participants go all out to create unforgettable ensembles. It's a visual feast that brings joy and awe to everyone lucky enough to witness it.

So, if you find yourself in San Francisco in May, make sure to mark Carnaval on your must-do list. Join the joyful crowds, immerse yourself in the vibrant culture, and experience the sheer exuberance of this incredible celebration. It's a time to embrace diversity, dance to your heart's content, and create memories that will last a lifetime. Get ready for a carnival like no other.

- Culture

Immerse yourself in the vibrant Latino culture that is deeply ingrained in the heart of The Mission. This neighborhood proudly embraces its roots, with early residents hailing from Mexico, Nicaragua, El Salvador, Guatemala, and beyond. So, why not fully embrace the cultural experience while you're here?

Prepare to indulge in a culinary adventure like no other. Taquerias are scattered on almost every corner, offering mouthwatering tacos that will transport your taste buds straight to Mexico. But the food scene doesn't stop there. You'll find food vendors dishing out delectable elotes (grilled corn on the cob smothered in delicious toppings) and pupusas (thick corn tortillas filled with savory ingredients) that will leave you craving more. The aromas alone will make your stomach rumble with anticipation!

As you stroll through The Mission, don't be surprised if you encounter street musicians serenading you with traditional mariachi or Banda songs. Their melodies add an enchanting atmosphere to the streets, making your experience even more memorable. Let the music guide your steps and embrace the rhythmic heartbeat of the neighborhood.

But the cultural immersion doesn't end with food and music. The Mission is also renowned for its stunning murals, many of which are heavily influenced by Latino culture. Every corner reveals vibrant artworks that tell stories of heritage, resilience, and unity. It's like walking through an outdoor art gallery, where each mural showcases the creativity and talent of local artists.

So, while you're here, make it a point to fully embrace the Latino culture that permeates The Mission. Indulge in the flavors of the street, let the music move your soul, and admire the incredible murals that bring the neighborhood to life. It's a journey of cultural exploration that will leave you with a deeper appreciation for the rich tapestry of diversity in San Francisco. Vamos a vivir la cultura Latina! (Let's live the Latino culture!)

Calling all art lovers! Get ready to explore the vibrant world of street art at the graffiti museum in the Mission. Marvel at the incredible talent displayed on the walls and immerse yourself in the creativity and expression of local artists. From colorful murals to thought-provoking pieces, the graffiti museum offers a unique and captivating experience. Don't forget to capture some Instagram-worthy shots and show your appreciation for this dynamic art form.

Get ready for some retail therapy and vibrant sights on Valencia Street in The Mission. Whether you're on the hunt for trendy threads from Taylor Stitch and Lululemon or have a penchant for vintage fashion, Valencia Street has got you covered.

As you stroll down this colorful street, get ready for a window-shopping extravaganza. Looking for that elusive vinyl record? Stranded Records is your go-to spot. Craving some indie books? Check out **Dog Eared Books** or **Borderland Books.**

Valencia Street's buildings are a feast for the eyes with their eye-popping colors. This vibrant motif is a common theme in The Mission, but it's especially noticeable here. Prepare for a visual treat that'll have you reaching for your camera.

Valencia Street is also a treasure trove of eclectic offerings. Discover taxidermy wonders or explore **Santería**, an Afro-Cuban folk religion. The street is filled with fascinating curiosities and hidden gems that cater to a wide range of interests.

And fear not, weary shoppers! When you've had your fill of browsing, there's no shortage of food and drink options to recharge your energy. Treat yourself to a delectable meal or grab a refreshing drink to rejuvenate.

Prepare your taste buds for an unforgettable culinary adventure in The Mission, where an incredible variety of food awaits. This neighborhood is a true melting pot, where greasy spoons and vibrant taquerias coexist with James Beard Award-winning restaurants. So, get ready to satisfy your cravings because The Mission has something for you.

When it comes to food, I always encourage people to start with the street vendors and charming mom-and-pop establishments. These hidden gems offer authentic flavors and a glimpse into the local food scene. But if you're in the mood for something a little more upscale, fear not! The Mission has got you covered too.

If you're in search of a truly exceptional dining experience, securing a reservation at **Lazy Bear** is a must. What began as a small pop-up restaurant has blossomed into a permanent fixture with two coveted Michelin stars. Prepare to be amazed by their innovative culinary creations that will tantalize your taste buds and leave you wanting more.

For a more laid-back vibe, make your way to **ABV**. This spot is a hidden gem known for serving up some of the juiciest and most delicious burgers in town. Sink your teeth into a mouthwatering burger and enjoy the relaxed atmosphere with friends or fellow food enthusiasts.

Now, let's talk about the iconic Mission-style Burrito. When that craving hits, head straight to **La Taqueria.** Since 1972, they've been crafting these burritos to perfection, and they've become a beloved institution in the neighborhood. Prepare yourself for a flavor explosion as you bite into the delicious and crispy goodness of their renowned burritos.

But The Mission doesn't stop at Mexican cuisine. You can also embark on a global culinary journey right here. Indulge in flavorful Thai dishes, savor the rich flavors of Pakistani cuisine, or explore the unique flavors of Burmese food. The options are truly endless, ensuring that you'll never go hungry while exploring this vibrant part of town.

So, come hungry and leave satisfied as you navigate the diverse food scene of The Mission. From street food delights to award-winning establishments, this neighborhood is a foodie's paradise. So, gather your friends, bring your appetite, and embark on a gastronomic adventure you won't soon forget. Bon appétit.

When the sun goes down, it's time to let loose and experience the Mission's vibrant nightlife. From trendy bars to lively clubs. Dance the night away to the beats of local DJs, sip craft cocktails, and make unforgettable memories with friends. Pro tip: Check out **Elbo Room, Make-Out Room**, or **El Techo** for a night filled with fun and good vibes.

## Nob Hill

Nob Hill has a history as grand as its mansions! Back in the late 19th century, this area was home to San Francisco's wealthiest residents, including railroad tycoons and industrialists. Their opulent mansions and luxurious hotels made Nob Hill the place to be. Sadly, the 1906 earthquake and fires destroyed much of the neighborhood's grandeur. But Nob Hill rose from the ashes, embodying resilience and elegance.

Situated in the heart of San Francisco, Nob Hill sits atop one of the city's famous seven hills. Get ready for stunning panoramic views of the Financial District, Union Square, and the Bay. Bounded by California Street to the north, Powell Street to the east, Bush Street to the south, and Mason Street to the west, Nob Hill is perfectly positioned for you to explore the city.

Ready to hit the streets of Nob Hill? Start with **California Street**, a main thoroughfare known for its iconic cable cars conquering those steep slopes. As you stroll along, you'll be mesmerized by the gorgeous Victorian homes and elegant apartment buildings. And if you're up for a taste of luxury, check out the high-end hotels, upscale shops, and gourmet restaurants that line California Street.

Another happening street in Nob Hill is **Polk Street**, buzzing with a lively mix of shops, boutiques, cafes, and bars. It's a hotspot for locals and visitors alike, offering a blend of trendy spots and hidden gems. And when the sun sets, Polk Street really comes alive with its vibrant nightlife scene. Get ready for a memorable night out on the town!

**Getting There**:

**By Cable Car**: Hop aboard the Powell-Hyde or Powell-Mason cable car lines that glide through Nob Hill. It's not just transportation; it's an iconic and scenic experience that will have you enjoying the ride up those hilly streets!

**By Bus**: Take advantage of the several bus lines serving Nob Hill, including the 1-California and 19-Polk. For detailed routes and schedules, check out the San Francisco Municipal Transportation Agency (SFMTA) website.

**By BART**: If you're coming from outside the city, hop on the BART and head to the Montgomery Street station. From there, you can transfer to a bus or take a pleasant walk to reach Nob Hill, depending on where you want to go within the neighborhood.

## Nob Hill Bucket List

- Grace Cathedral

Get ready to be blown away by the sheer beauty and welcoming spirit of Grace Cathedral, a true gem that has been captivating visitors since the swinging 60s (even though it took decades to construct). This Nob Hill landmark will leave you in awe with its grandeur and intricate details. As the third largest Episcopal Cathedral in the U.S., it's a French Gothic masterpiece that will take your breath away.

Picture twin towers soaring towards the sky, adorned with stunning stained glass windows showcasing over 1,100 figures. It's like stepping into a fairytale. But here's the best part—Grace Cathedral is not just about architecture; it's about embracing people from all walks of life. You'll feel a sense of extreme openness and inclusivity as soon as you step foot inside.

Prepare yourself for a visual feast. From the replica doors of Ghiberti's "Gates of Paradise" to the awe-inspiring Keith Haring AIDS Chapel altarpiece, every corner of the cathedral holds a treasure waiting to be discovered. Take a meditative stroll through both the indoor and outdoor labyrinths, allowing your mind to wander and find tranquility. Marvel at the displayed works by the cathedral's resident artist, adding a touch of contemporary art to the mix.

Grace Cathedral is not just a place for quiet contemplation. It's a hub of activity and cultural expression. Attend invigorating yoga sessions, sway to the rhythms of jazz concerts, or even let loose at the occasional dance party. This place knows how to blend spirituality with a vibrant and lively atmosphere.

Want to delve deeper into the cathedral's rich history and architecture? Look no further than the available tours and embark on a captivating walk through time, unraveling the secrets and stories that have shaped this extraordinary place.

So, get ready to have your senses dazzled at Grace Cathedral. It's a sanctuary of beauty, inclusivity, and cultural exploration. Let its stunning architecture, mesmerizing art, and engaging events ignite your spirit and leave you with memories that will last a lifetime. Don't forget to bring your curiosity and an open heart as you embark on this unforgettable journey through time and spirituality.

- Nob Hill Cafe

Just a stone's throw away from the magnificent Grace Cathedral, you'll discover the delightful Nob Hill Cafe, a cozy Italian eatery that will warm your heart and satisfy your cravings with its generous bowls of pasta and mouth watering

Tuscan-style dishes. It's the perfect spot for a comforting and flavorful meal that will transport you straight to Italy.

If you're in the mood for some unpretentious and delectable seafood, make sure to swing by **Swan Oyster Depot** on Polk Street. This legendary counter has been serving eager patrons for over a century, dishing out the freshest catches from the sea. Prepare your taste buds for a true seafood extravaganza that will leave you wanting more.

For a touch of elegance and a dose of California nostalgia, head over to the iconic **Big 4 restaurant**, nestled on the ground floor of the Huntington Hotel. Step into a world of sophistication as you sink into the plush green booths, admire the crisp white tablecloths, and immerse yourself in the extensive collection of California memorabilia that adorns the walls. And let's not forget about the hearty and satisfying entrees that await you, such as the succulent braised boneless short ribs and the comforting chicken pot pie. To add to the ambiance, there's even a piano player serenading you every evening, creating an atmosphere of refined charm.

But the fun doesn't end there! If you're ready to unleash your inner superstar, head on over to **The Mint Karaoke Lounge**, a neighborhood gem where you can belt out your favorite tunes and become the star of the night. Gather your friends, choose your favorite songs, and get ready for a memorable and entertaining karaoke experience that will have you singing your heart out.

- SF Masonic Auditorium

Get ready to enter a world of mystery and music at Nob Hill's iconic SF Masonic Auditorium. This historic venue holds a dual identity: it serves as a meeting place for the California Freemasons, a fraternal organization dating back to the Gold Rush era, and as an awe-inspiring concert venue affectionately known as "The Masonic."

Step into this extraordinary space, operated by Live Nation, and prepare to be amazed. With a capacity of 3,300 seats spread across multiple tiers, The Masonic offers a one-of-a-kind setting for live performances. It underwent a fabulous renovation in 2014, transforming it into a modern masterpiece. Picture dazzling new lighting, captivating art installations, and a state-of-the-art sound system that will transport you into a realm of auditory bliss.

Here, the music comes alive, enveloping you in a complete sensory experience. Whether you prefer to rock out in the general admission area or relax in a seated section, The Masonic has got you covered. It's a venue that caters to all, ensuring that every concert is an unforgettable event.

And let's talk about the incredible lineup of acts that grace The Masonic's stage. Prepare to be entertained by renowned performers from various genres. Tenacious D brings their rock and comedic genius, Chelsea Handler serves up laughter with her wit and charm, and the hilarious SF-native Ali Wong will have you in stitches. These are just a taste of the incredible talent that awaits you at this phenomenal venue.

So, mark your calendars and get ready to immerse yourself in the magic of The Masonic. This historic meeting space turned sensational concert hall offers an unforgettable experience that combines rich tradition with modern entertainment. Get your tickets, gather your friends, and get ready to create memories that will last a lifetime as you enjoy an unforgettable performance at The Masonic.

- Cable Car Museum

Get ready to embark on a journey through time and uncover the fascinating world of San Francisco's iconic cable cars at the Cable Car Museum. This incredible museum, located right along the Powell/Mason cable car line, is a true celebration of local history and an absolute must-visit.

Step inside and get ready to be amazed by the stories and artifacts that await you. Learn all about Andrew Smith Hallidie, the visionary who revolutionized transportation with the world's very first cable car. Discover how these magnificent machines once traversed the city, with 23 different cable car lines weaving through the streets (although today we're down to three).

The Cable Car Museum showcases the impressive machinery that powers these beloved cable cars. Marvel at the massive engines and intricate winding wheels that work tirelessly to keep the cables in motion. Immerse yourself in the past through historic photographs that bring the golden age of cable cars to life. You'll also have the opportunity to explore mechanical devices like grips and brake mechanisms, which play a crucial role in the operation of these iconic vehicles. And don't forget to take a closer look at the three antique cable cars on display, a true treat for any history enthusiast.

But the adventure doesn't end there! The museum even has an on-site shop where you can purchase authentic cable car bells. Imagine taking home a piece of San Francisco's iconic charm and adding a touch of nostalgia to your own life.

- Tonga Room & Hurricane Bar,

When you gaze at the magnificent Fairmont Hotel, it's hard to believe that hidden away on its lower level lies a legendary tiki bar that has been captivating guests for decades. Welcome to the Tonga Room & Hurricane Bar, one of the oldest and most iconic tiki bars in the entire country. Prepare to be transported to a tropical oasis right in the heart of San Francisco.

Back in 1945, this enchanting spot emerged from the transformation of a beloved indoor swimming pool that attracted celebrities and hotel guests alike. With the expertise of a former MGM set designer, the Tonga Room was born, featuring a mesmerizing Polynesian theme that instantly transports you to paradise. Imagine yourself surrounded by a central "lagoon," where simulated tropical rainstorms create an immersive experience complete with thunder and lightning. Canoes gracefully hang from the ceiling, and the dance floor is crafted from salvaged wood from a historic schooner. As you soak in the ambiance, you'll be treated to live performances by the talented Island Grove Band, belting out all your favorite Top 40 hits from a thatch-covered floating barge.

While the Tonga Room offers a delightful array of dishes, including mouthwatering cashew shrimp and flavorful kung pao chicken, it's the expertly crafted cocktails that truly steal the show. Indulge in the rum-infused delights of Mai Tais and Fog Cutters, signature concoctions that have become beloved favorites among visitors. Sip on these tropical elixirs and let the worries of the world melt away as you bask in the vibrant atmosphere and the company of friends.

The Tonga Room & Hurricane Bar is a destination that transports you to a bygone era of tropical indulgence and exotic charm. It's the perfect place to escape reality, embrace the spirit of aloha, and create unforgettable memories. So, gather your friends, put on your Hawaiian shirt, and embark on a thrilling adventure that will leave you enchanted and longing for more.

- Top of the Mark

No visit to Nob Hill in San Francisco is complete without a stop at the legendary Top of the Mark. This penthouse-level cocktail bar and lounge has been wowing guests since its grand opening in 1939, and it continues to captivate with its breathtaking views and timeless charm. Prepare to be transported to a world of sophistication and elegance as you indulge in a wide array of martini variations that will leave your taste buds tingling.

But it's not just the martinis that make Top of the Mark a true gem. This place is steeped in local lore and history, adding an extra layer of intrigue to your experience. Take a stroll to the northwest corner, lovingly dubbed "Weeper's Corner," where during World War II, women would gather to bid farewell to their loved ones as they embarked on their military service. The emotional moments shared here created lasting memories and earned the spot its poignant nickname. You'll also discover a collection of "squadron bottles," a tradition that originated during the Korean War and serves as a tribute to the brave servicemen and women who served their country.

For an unforgettable experience, time your visit to Top of the Mark around sunset. As the sun descends below the horizon, the sky becomes a magnificent canvas of fiery hues. Witness the transformation as shades of red and pink paint the heavens, casting a magical glow over the city. It's a truly mesmerizing sight that will take your breath away.

So, raise a glass to the rich history, breathtaking views, and the vibrant spirit of San Francisco at Top of the Mark. Savor the moment, sip on a perfectly crafted martini, and let the enchantment of this iconic destination sweep you off your feet. Cheers to unforgettable experiences and unforgettable views.

## Pacific Heights

Welcome to Pacific Heights, one of San Francisco's poshest neighborhoods with a captivating history that goes way back to the late 19th century. Originally called "Black Point" for its dark cliffs, this place went through a major transformation in the late 1800s and became the stunning Pacific Heights we know today. The name change reflects its elevated position and jaw-dropping views of the Pacific Ocean and San Francisco Bay.

Back in the late 19th and early 20th centuries, Pacific Heights was the place to be for the city's wealthiest folks. They built magnificent mansions along the picturesque tree-lined streets, many of which still stand proudly today. These homes come in all sorts of architectural styles, from Victorian to

Beaux-Arts and Italianate, showing off the opulence and grandeur of that golden era.

Pacific Heights sits pretty in the northern part of San Francisco, boasting a prime spot overlooking the city and the bay. It's bordered by Presidio Avenue to the west, Broadway to the north, Van Ness Avenue to the east, and Pacific Avenue to the south. Being up high means you get to feast your eyes on awe-inspiring views of the Golden Gate Bridge, Alcatraz Island, and the city skyline. Prepare to be amazed!

Now, let's explore the best streets Pacific Heights has to offer. First up, we have the famous **"Billionaires' Row"** on Broadway. This iconic street is home to some of San Francisco's most lavish mansions, complete with exquisite architectural details and vistas that will leave you breathless.

Next on the list is **Fillmore Street**, known for its vibrant atmosphere. It's a hub of upscale shops, trendy boutiques, art galleries, and fantastic dining spots. Whether you're looking to indulge in a shopping spree or savor some scrumptious food, Fillmore Street has got you covered.

If you're craving a taste of elegance and tranquility, head over to **Vallejo Street**. This charming street is lined with elegant Victorian homes, offering a serene ambiance and picturesque views that capture the true essence of Pacific Heights.

**Getting There**

Hop on a bus! Pacific Heights is well-served by various bus lines, including the 3-Jackson, 22-Fillmore, and 24-Divisadero. Check out the San Francisco Municipal Transportation Agency (SFMTA) website or their mobile apps for detailed bus routes and schedules.

For a touch of historic charm, you can jump aboard the California Street cable car line. This iconic mode of transportation runs along the northern edge of Pacific Heights, treating you to a scenic ride while experiencing a piece of San Francisco's history.

Of course, ride-sharing services like Uber and Lyft are widely available in the city, so you can easily request a ride to Pacific Heights whenever you fancy.

- Lyon Street Steps

Head on over to the top of the Lyon Street Steps, or if you're up for a good workout, start from the bottom and climb your way up. Either way, get ready for some jaw-dropping views. From here, you'll be treated to sweeping vistas of the magnificent Presidio, the iconic Golden Gate Bridge, the picturesque Marin Headlands, and you might even catch a glimpse of Alcatraz in the distance. It's like having a postcard-worthy panorama right at your fingertips.

- San Francisco Jewish Community Center (JCC).

Make sure to swing by the San Francisco Jewish Community Center (JCC). This vibrant hub is a hot spot for mind-bending performance art, live concerts, engaging talks, and captivating art exhibits. The JCC is a favorite among locals, so you know you're in for a treat. Who knows, you might discover your new favorite artist or catch a mesmerizing performance that will leave you in awe.

- Broadway

Take a leisurely stroll east along Broadway and prepare to be amazed by the opulent mansions that line the famous Billionaire's Row in Pacific Heights. It's like stepping into a world of luxury and grandeur! As you wander along, keep an eye out for a special house that might ring a bell—it's the very same house featured in Bay Area native Robin Williams' beloved movie "Mrs. Doubtfire." It's a fun little nod to cinematic history right in the heart of Pacific Heights.

Feeling in need of a caffeine fix? Make a pit stop at the renowned **Blue Bottle Coffee,** a local company that has now made its mark globally. Savor their expertly crafted coffee and fuel up for the rest of your adventure.

Next up, head to Alta Plaza Park, where you can bask in the beauty of this elevated green oasis. Find a cozy spot on one of the park's inviting benches and take in the stunning downtown view that stretches out before you. If you look closely, you'll catch a glimpse of the exquisite French Classical style of the Spreckels Mansion, known for its intricate scrollwork. To get an up-close look at this architectural gem, make your way to the corner of Washington and Octavia. But remember, it's a private home rumored to be owned by the celebrity romance writer Danielle Steel, so resist the temptation to ring the doorbell and simply admire its splendor from the sidewalk.

Make sure to include a visit to Japantown on your San Francisco itinerary. This vibrant neighborhood is a foodie paradise, offering a delightful array of beloved eateries, restaurants, and sweet shops that will leave your taste buds jumping with joy.

Prepare to be amazed by the variety of culinary delights Japantown has to offer. Satisfy your sushi cravings at the top-notch sushi joints scattered throughout the area. For an extraordinary dining experience, head to Oma San Francisco Station and indulge in their Michelin-starred omakase. And if you're up for a bit of excitement, check out Hikari Sushi & Bar, where sushi is served to you via a cool bullet train. It's a sushi experience that both adults and kids will find thrilling!

Craving some Korean barbecue? Look no further than Daeho Kalbijjim or Seoul Garden, where you can grill up some mouthwatering meats and savor the authentic flavors of Korean cuisine.

For a whimsical treat, make a beeline to Belly Good Café & Crepes, where you can delight in crepes topped with adorable edible animals. It's like having an edible art piece on your plate!

Ready for a fusion adventure? Don't miss out on the sushi burritos at Kui Shin Bo, a delightful blend of Japanese and Mexican cuisines that will surely satisfy your cravings. And if you're in the mood for some modern Thai cuisine, head over to Nari inside Hotel Kabuki. They serve up innovative Thai dishes with a contemporary twist that will tantalize your taste buds.

- Fillmore Street

Take your time and enjoy a leisurely stroll once you reach Fillmore Street, located on the western edge of Japantown. This bustling street is a shopaholic's dream, teeming with boutique shops and eateries that offer a delightful mix of local and international treasures.

Prepare to be captivated by the wide range of shops lining Fillmore Street. If you're a fan of exquisite jewelry, be sure to visit Trabert Goldsmiths, where you'll find stunning pieces that will add a touch of sparkle to your collection. For unique and stylish housewares, make a stop at Jonathan Adler and Nest, where you'll discover a treasure trove of beautiful and functional items for your home.

Bookworms and vintage enthusiasts will be in paradise with **Browser Books** and **Mureta & Co.** These establishments offer a delightful selection of antique and vintage jewelry, along with an impressive collection of books that will satisfy any avid reader's cravings.

What makes Fillmore Street truly special is its ability to seamlessly blend local favorites with international powerhouses. You'll find clothing and shoes from beloved local brands like Margaret O'Leary and Cuyana, effortlessly coexisting with renowned international fashion giants like Intermix and Rag & Bone. It's a fashion lover's paradise, where you can explore the best of both worlds.

When it comes to dining and drinking, the bars and restaurants along Fillmore Street and its neighboring side streets in Pacific Heights are where the magic happens. Prepare your taste buds for a delightful culinary adventure!

A must-visit establishment is the iconic Harry's Bar, a timeless gem with its classic ambiance, cozy bar stools, and rich dark wood fixtures. Pull up a seat, lean on the brass rail, and join the local crowd as they indulge in martinis and savor delicious beef sliders. It's the perfect spot to see and be seen while enjoying classic favorites.

As you explore further, you'll discover a world of flavors waiting to be explored. Turkish delights await you at Troya, where you can savor the aromas and tastes of authentic Turkish cuisine. Transport yourself to the Mediterranean at Noosh, where you can indulge in delectable dishes that will make your taste buds dance with joy.

Craving Vietnamese flavors? Look no further than Bunmee, where you can sink your teeth into mouth watering banh mi sandwiches and other Vietnamese culinary delights. For a casual Mexican feast, Tacobar is the place to be, serving up a variety of tasty Mexican dishes that will satisfy your cravings.

But let's not forget the true star of the show: SPQR, the Italian restaurant that has earned a Michelin star for an impressive 10 years in a row. Prepare to be wowed by their exquisite Italian creations, crafted with precision and passion. It's a dining experience that will take your taste buds on a journey through the flavors of Italy.

- Lower Pacific Heights

Lower Pacific Heights is the place to be if you're looking for a lively and vibrant atmosphere in San Francisco. Get ready to experience the funky and jazzy side of the neighborhood in the Fillmore District. The Fillmore and the Boom Boom Room have been rocking the local music scene for ages, drawing crowds with their live performances and dance-worthy beats. Prepare to let loose and groove to the rhythm of the night!

For a diverse musical experience that spans genres and styles from all around the world, make your way to The

Independent. Located on Divisadero Street, this entertainment hub attracts a global audience with its impressive lineup of musicians, DJs, and musical acts. Get ready to dance, sing along, and lose yourself in the electrifying energy of the crowd.

During the day, the corner of Fillmore and Geary comes to life with its own unique charm. Start your day at The Social Study, where you can fuel up with a delicious cup of coffee. But wait, there's more! As the day transitions into night, this place transforms into a hip bar, complete with beats, movies, and live DJ sets on the weekends. It's the perfect spot to unwind, enjoy good company, and sip on your favorite libations.

When it comes to satisfying your taste buds, here are my top recs in Lower Pacific Heights. Treat yourself to an incredible seafood experience at The Anchovy Bar, where you can indulge in the freshest local catches. For a truly unique dining adventure, check out State Bird Provisions, known for its California cuisine that celebrates the flavors of the region. And don't forget to stop by The Progress, where you'll find delicious dishes that showcase the best of local ingredients and culinary expertise.

## Presidio

The Presidio, located in San Francisco, has a rich history that spans several centuries. Originally established as a Spanish military fort in 1776, it served as a strategic outpost during the early days of San Francisco's colonization. Over the years, it transitioned into a U.S. Army post, playing a significant role in various military campaigns and conflicts. Today, the Presidio stands as a remarkable national park and a testament to its historical significance.

Geographically, the Presidio is situated at the northern tip of the San Francisco Peninsula, bordered by the Golden Gate Bridge to the north and the Pacific Ocean to the west. It covers an expansive area of over 1,500 acres, encompassing rolling hills, lush forests, picturesque coastal areas, and stunning views of the surrounding natural beauty.

**Lincoln Boulevard**: This scenic road offers breathtaking views of the Golden Gate Bridge and the Pacific Ocean. It winds through the heart of the Presidio, passing by historic landmarks, art installations, and beautiful natural landscapes.

**Main Post**: Located at the heart of the Presidio, the Main Post area features a collection of historic buildings, including the Presidio Officers' Club, the Visitor Center, and the Walt Disney Family Museum. It's a great place to learn about the Presidio's history and engage in cultural activities.

**Crissy Field**: While not technically a street, Crissy Field is a picturesque waterfront area that attracts visitors with its expansive green spaces, sandy beaches, and stunning views of the Golden Gate Bridge. It's perfect for leisurely walks, picnics, and enjoying outdoor recreational activities.

Getting to the Presidio is convenient using public transportation. Here are a few options:

**Bus**: The Presidio is served by several bus lines, including the PresidiGo Shuttle, which offers free transportation within the park. You can also use Muni bus lines such as the 28 and 43 to access different parts of the Presidio.

**PresidioGo**: The PresidioGo Shuttle provides free transportation from downtown San Francisco to various destinations within the Presidio, including the Main Post and Crissy Field. Check the Presidio's website for the shuttle's schedule and stops.

**Biking/Walking:** If you're in the nearby areas, biking or walking to the Presidio can be a pleasant option. The park has bike-friendly paths and walking trails that allow you to enjoy the natural surroundings and easily explore different areas.

## Presidio Bucket List

- Visitor center

Make sure to swing by the visitor center, located right on the Main Post of the Presidio. It's like the "front door" to this amazing park! This newly opened facility is the perfect place to kick off your day of exploration. The friendly staff is there to greet you and help you make the most of your visit.

Inside the visitor center, you'll find interactive exhibits, maps, and videos that will give you a fantastic introduction to the Presidio. Dive into the park's fascinating history and learn about the incredible events and activities that await you here. You'll also get practical tips on how to navigate the park using the convenient and free PresidiGo Shuttle.

Make your way to the southern entrance of the Golden Gate Bridge, right here in the Presidio San Francisco. It's the perfect starting point for your Golden Gate Bridge adventure! Take a leisurely stroll along the eastern side of the bridge, marveling at the iconic structure as you go. Don't forget to check out the small outdoor museum to learn even more about the bridge's history. And if you're feeling hungry, grab a quick bite to eat at one of the nearby spots.

Make a stop at the Golden Gate Bridge Welcome Center while you're here. Step inside and you'll be greeted with a treasure trove of goodies and souvenirs all about the Golden Gate Bridge. It's the perfect place to pick up a memento to remember your visit. The friendly staff is also there to assist you with any questions you may have or provide directions to make sure you have the best experience possible. Plus, if you're relying on public transportation, you'll be pleased to know that the SF Muni bus station is conveniently located right here at the Welcome Center.

- Hiking Trails

The Presidio offers a plethora of hiking trails that will take you on a scenic adventure with stunning views of the Golden Gate Bridge. Lace up your walking shoes, pick a trail, and immerse yourself in the beauty of this iconic landmark.

Get ready for an exciting adventure by joining a guided tour in the Presidio San Francisco! There are plenty of options to choose from, catering to different interests and preferences. Let's explore a few of them:

- Free Walking Tours

Inside the Presidio, you'll discover a variety of walking tours that showcase the park's natural beauty, art installations, and more. Best of all, most of these tours are free! Check out the Presidio's calendar to see which walks are scheduled during your visit. Whether you're into nature or art, there's a tour for everyone.

- City Tour

Hop aboard a luxury motor coach and embark on a comprehensive 3.5-hour tour that covers all the top sights of San Francisco, including the iconic Presidio. This daily tour departs at 8:40 am and takes you to must-see locations like Twin Peaks, Chinatown, North Beach, and of course, the Presidio San Francisco. Sit back, relax, and enjoy the sights as your knowledgeable guide shares fascinating stories along the way.

- Fire Engine Tour

Buckle up for an unforgettable experience on this small-group tour aboard an open-air vintage red fire truck. The adventure begins in Fisherman's Wharf and takes you through the Presidio San Francisco, with a stop at Fort Point. You'll then cruise over the magnificent Golden Gate Bridge before returning to your starting point. During this 90-minute tour, you'll learn all about these top SF attractions while enjoying the thrill of riding in a fire truck.

- GoCar Tour, Golden Gate Bridge & Lombard Loop

Have you spotted those small, yellow, two-seater cars zooming around the city? Now it's your turn to take the wheel! Embark on the Golden Gate Bridge & Lombard Loop in a GoCar. These nifty cars provide an audio guide that will navigate you through the route, allowing you to explore top attractions, including the Presidio San Francisco, at your own pace. Feel free to make stops along the way to snap photos and soak in the sights.

With these guided tours, you'll have the opportunity to delve deeper into the wonders of the Presidio San Francisco and its surrounding attractions. Whether you prefer walking, riding in a luxury motor coach, an open-air fire truck, or even driving a GoCar, there's a tour that suits your style. So grab your sense of adventure and get ready to explore the Presidio in a whole new way!

- Batteries

Get ready to dive into the military history of the Presidio San Francisco! Throughout the park, you'll discover a total of

17-gun batteries that played a crucial role in protecting the Golden Gate Strait when the Presidio was an active Army Base. These batteries, stocked with ammunition and manned by soldiers, were a formidable defense system.

During your visit, be sure to explore some of the well-preserved batteries that are still standing. They provide a fascinating glimpse into the past and make for a fun adventure. Let's highlight a few of them:

To the west of the Golden Gate Bridge, you'll find four batteries lined up along the coast: Cranston, Godfrey, Crosby, and Chamberlin (in that order from east to west). Battery Chamberlin is a standout, as it houses a massive 50-ton, six-inch diameter "disappearing gun." This incredible piece of artillery will leave you in awe. For an extra treat, mark your calendars for the first full weekend of each month from 11 am to 3 pm, when the National Park Service offers demonstrations of the gun. They'll happily answer any questions you may have and provide a truly immersive experience.

On the eastern side of the Golden Gate Bridge, make sure to visit Battery East Vista. This fantastic vista point underwent renovation in 2015, and it now offers jaw-dropping views of the Golden Gate Bridge and the beautiful expanse of the SF Bay. Prepare to be amazed as you soak in the stunning sights and capture memorable photos.

As you explore these gun batteries, you'll not only witness their impressive architecture and engineering but also gain a deeper understanding of the Presidio's military significance. It's a chance to step back in time and appreciate the historical legacy that shaped this remarkable place.

- Marshall's Beach

Get ready to discover the hidden gem of Marshall's Beach! While it may not have all the bells and whistles, this beach is a true treasure, offering spectacular vistas of the iconic Golden Gate Bridge, the glistening bay waters, and the picturesque Marin Headlands.

As you make your way to Marshall's Beach, leave your expectations for amenities behind and embrace the natural beauty that surrounds you. This is a place to escape the hustle and bustle of the city, unwind, and let the stunning scenery take center stage.

Picture yourself basking in the warm sun or strolling along the sandy shoreline while gazing at the majestic Golden Gate Bridge. The views are simply breathtaking, and you'll find yourself mesmerized by the panoramic sights that stretch before you.

While you won't find shops or cafes here, that's part of the charm. Marshall's Beach offers a serene and tranquil atmosphere, inviting you to connect with nature and find inner peace. It's the perfect spot for a peaceful picnic or a moment of quiet contemplation.

While exploring Marshall's Beach, it's worth noting that you may encounter a small number of sunbathers enjoying the beach in the nude. It's a popular spot for those who prefer a clothing-optional experience. If you're planning to visit with children or prefer a more traditional beach environment, it's important to be aware of this aspect and make an informed decision.

- Baker Beach

Just a stone's throw away from Marshall's Beach, you'll discover another fantastic sandy retreat called Baker Beach. It's conveniently located right off the Coastal Trail, and there are a few access points, including the famous Sand Ladder where you can descend to the beach.

Baker Beach is a local favorite for several reasons. First off, it's quite spacious, giving you plenty of room to spread out and enjoy the coastal ambiance. Plus, the views are simply breathtaking in every direction. Whether you're gazing out at the majestic ocean waves or marveling at the stunning cityscape, this beach offers a visual feast for the eyes.

Now, let's be real—San Francisco isn't exactly known for its beach weather. That's why Baker Beach serves more as a recreational haven for locals than a traditional sunbathing and swimming hotspot. You'll often find residents using this sandy expanse as a gathering spot to hang out with friends, go for leisurely walks, or even bring their furry friends for a refreshing doggy frolic.

So, while you may not find hordes of sunseekers in their swimsuits, Baker Beach still provides a charming coastal escape where you can soak up the relaxed vibes and appreciate the natural beauty of San Francisco's shoreline. Don't forget your camera because the picturesque vistas are definitely worth capturing.

Just a hop, skip, and a jump away from Crissy Field on the eastern side of the Golden Gate Bridge, you'll stumble upon the Military Intelligence Service History Learning Center. This little gem of a museum takes you on a captivating journey through the WWII history of Japanese Americans who played a vital role in the Army and were residing in this very building when the infamous attack on Pearl Harbor occurred.

Prepare to be immersed in their compelling story as the museum delves into their pre-attack responsibilities and the tumultuous events that unfolded when orders were given for the mass internment of approximately 120,000 Japanese Americans along the West Coast.

Ready to plan your visit? The Military Intelligence Service History Learning Center warmly welcomes visitors on weekends from 12 pm to 5 pm. The entrance fee is $10 per person, but hold on, there are some sweet perks too! Veterans and kids under 12 can enter for free, so don't forget to bring your little ones or show your military pride.

Located at 640 Mason Street, this intriguing museum is just waiting to transport you back in time and shed light on an important chapter in American history. So mark it on your map, gather your friends or family, and get ready to embark on an educational adventure that will leave you with a deeper appreciation for the courage and resilience of the Japanese American community during those challenging times.

Right along the picturesque Crissy Field, there are three exciting indoor activities that are sure to keep your kids entertained and energized!

First up, we have the House of **Air Trampoline Park** (926 Mason), where your little ones can bounce, flip, and soar to their heart's content. With a sea of trampolines at their disposal, they'll be leaping with joy and laughter all afternoon long.

Next on the list is the **Batter's Box** (933 Mason), a haven for aspiring sluggers. Inside, they'll find indoor batting cages where they can practice their swing and unleash their inner baseball superstar. It's a home run for sure!

Last but not least, we have **Planet Granite** (924 Mason), an indoor climbing gym that will take their adventurous spirits to new heights. With walls designed for climbers of all skill levels, they'll have a blast scaling the heights and conquering challenges like true rock stars.

- Walt Disney Family Museum

Step into the magical world of Walt Disney at the Walt Disney Family Museum. This isn't your typical amusement park, but an extraordinary journey that delves into the life and legacy of the man behind the beloved characters and enchanting stories.

Prepare to be captivated as you learn fascinating details about Walt Disney himself, his family, and the extraordinary business empire he built. Explore his inspiring life through personal photos and rare family memorabilia that you won't find anywhere else. Discover the incredible vision and determination that led to the creation of one of the most successful entertainment companies in the world.

Calling all die-hard Disney enthusiasts! Get ready to geek out over exclusive artifacts like the impressive 13-foot model of the original Disneyland, offering a glimpse into Walt's dream come to life. And don't miss the opportunity to see the first-known drawing of the iconic Mickey Mouse, a historic piece of Disney magic.

But that's not all! The museum goes above and beyond with guest speakers who share their insights, and they even treat visitors to classic Disney movie screenings each month. It's an immersive experience that will make you feel like a kid again.

- Presidio Theatre

Discover a hidden gem nestled in the heart of the Presidio of San Francisco - the Presidio Theatre! This intimate performing arts center may be small, with just 600 seats, but it packs a big punch when it comes to entertainment.

Prepare to be dazzled as the theater comes alive with a diverse range of shows throughout the year. From captivating plays to enchanting musical performances, there's something for everyone to enjoy. Whether you're a fan of drama, comedy, dance, or live music, the Presidio Theatre has it all.

Immerse yourself in the vibrant atmosphere as talented performers take the stage and transport you to a world of artistry and creativity. The cozy setting creates an intimate connection between the audience and the performers, making every show an immersive and memorable experience.

Keep an eye on the theater's schedule to catch the latest productions and performances. You never know what hidden treasures await you at the Presidio Theatre - it's a cultural hub that brings the community together through the power of the performing arts.

- Cafe RX

Start your day off right at Cafe RX, a fantastic spot for a casual and delicious breakfast or lunch. Located at 1013 Torney Ave, this charming café is open weekdays from 7 am to 2:30 pm, serving up a variety of mouthwatering treats. Indulge in their scrumptious bagels, sandwiches, and salads that are sure to satisfy your cravings. What sets this place apart is the owner's Salvadoran heritage, which brings a delightful Latin twist to the menu. So, get ready to embark on a flavor-packed journey that combines the best of both worlds!

- Arguello

If you're craving Mexican cuisine with a modern twist, look no further than Arguello. This vibrant restaurant is the place to be for a delightful lunch, dinner, or happy hour experience. Swing by Wednesday to Friday from 11 am to 9 pm, Saturday from 11 am to 3 pm & 4 pm to 9 pm, and Sunday & Tuesday from 11 am to 4 pm. Located within the Presidio Officer's

Club at 50 Moraga Ave, Arguello will tantalize your taste buds with their delectable Mexican dishes. From traditional favorites to innovative creations, there's something for everyone to enjoy. So, gather your amigos and get ready for a fiesta of flavors!

- Presidio Social Club

Prepare yourself for a memorable dining experience at the hidden gem known as the Presidio Social Club. Nestled within the Presidio San Francisco at 563 Ruger St, this charming establishment serves up fresh and delectable California cuisine that will leave you craving more. Whether you're joining them for lunch, dinner, or their famous weekend brunch, you're in for a treat. Indulge in their tantalizing menu options, such as the mouthwatering salmon pizza, the delightful Dungeness Crab Louis sandwich, or the irresistible gourmet mac and cheese. While most of the seating is indoors, make sure to request a spot outside if the sun is shining. The patio may be small, but it offers a lovely setting for a delightful lunch or dinner experience. So, don't miss out on this culinary haven and get ready to savor the flavors of California at the Presidio Social Club.

## SoMa

SoMa, short for South of Market, is bursting with life, history, and creativity. It has come a long way from its industrial roots to become a thriving hub of innovation, technology, and arts.

In the old days, SoMa was all about warehouses, factories, and railroad yards. But in the 90s, it got a major makeover and became the place to be for tech companies, startups, and cultural institutions. Now, you'll find a mix of sleek high-rise buildings, hip lofts, and charming historical structures that tell the story of its industrial past.

Let's talk about the streets. Folsom Street is a happening hotspot that stretches from the Embarcadero to 13th Street. It's packed with cool bars, trendy nightclubs, and mouthwatering restaurants, making it a paradise for nightlife lovers. Another bustling street is **Howard Street**, famous for its lively traffic and its proximity to the legendary Moscone Center, where exciting conventions take place.

Getting to SoMa using public transportation is a breeze. You've got options galore! Hop on buses, light rail, or subway lines that conveniently serve the neighborhood. Start your journey at the Powell Street BART station near Union Square, and from there, you can catch Muni Metro lines or buses along Market Street to reach SoMa. If you're coming from the South Bay, the Caltrain Station at Fourth and King Streets is your direct gateway to this vibrant neighborhood.

Of course, walking or biking is a fantastic way to explore SoMa too. The neighborhood is compact and pedestrian-friendly, with bike lanes and shared paths that make getting around a joy. So put on your comfy shoes or rent a bike, and let the adventure begin!

SoMa isn't just about technology and innovation; it's also a cultural treasure trove. Get ready to be wowed by world-class museums like the San Francisco Museum of Modern Art (SFMOMA) and the Contemporary Jewish Museum. Make sure to visit the beautiful Yerba Buena Gardens, right in the heart of SoMa. Here, you'll find lush green spaces, awe-inspiring views, captivating public art, and the fabulous Yerba Buena Center for the Arts.

## SoMa Bucket List

- Salesforce Park

Get ready to explore Salesforce Park, one of the coolest attractions in San Francisco! This public park is unlike anything you've seen before. Picture this: it's located on top of the Salesforce Transit Center, and you can even reach it by taking a fun and scenic gondola ride. How awesome is that?

Salesforce Park is owned by the legendary software company from Silicon Valley, and it's a sprawling green oasis that sits 70 feet above ground, stretching across four blocks in SoMa. It's a remarkable feat of urban planning and design that will leave you in awe.

Once you step foot in Salesforce Park, you'll be greeted by a lush and vibrant landscape. Take a leisurely stroll along the paved trails, surrounded by beautiful plants and trees. Find a cozy spot to relax, maybe enjoy a picnic or read a book while soaking up the California sunshine.

The park also hosts various events and activities throughout the year, from live music performances to art installations.

Keep an eye on their calendar to see what exciting happenings await you during your visit.

And did we mention the breathtaking views? From Salesforce Park, you'll be treated to panoramic vistas of the city skyline, including iconic landmarks like the Transamerica Pyramid. It's the perfect spot to snap some envy-inducing photos for your Instagram feed.

Get ready for an art-filled adventure at the San Francisco Museum of Modern Art (SFMOMA) in SoMa! This museum is a true gem, not just in the neighborhood, but in the entire city. It's a must-visit for art enthusiasts and those looking to immerse themselves in creative brilliance.

Inside SFMOMA, you'll discover a vast collection of artworks that will leave you in awe. From paintings to sculptures and everything in between, there's something for everyone to appreciate. Get ready to encounter the masterpieces of renowned artists like Andy Warhol, Diego Rivera, Rene Magritte, and Frida Kahlo. The museum showcases contemporary art that pushes boundaries and sparks imagination.

The SFMOMA is not just a museum; it's an experience. Prepare to spend an entire day exploring its multiple levels, each offering a unique perspective on different mediums of art. With every step you take, you'll discover new wonders that will captivate your senses and ignite your creativity.

- Children's Creativity Museum

If you're visiting with kids, make sure to check out the Children's Creativity Museum right next door. This dedicated space is a haven for young minds, blending art and fun in the most delightful way. Your little ones will be thrilled by the interactive activities available, from music stations to robotics and even an animation studio. It's a fantastic opportunity for them to express their creativity and learn in a hands-on environment.

And don't forget the outdoor playground! The Children's Creativity Museum has a charming playground with a carousel, perfect for letting the kids burn off some energy while enjoying the fresh air.

- Moscone Center

Get ready to immerse yourself in the excitement of events and expos at the fabulous Moscone Center in Yerba Buena! This state-of-the-art building is not just a venue, it's a destination in itself.

Take a moment to admire the stunning facade of Moscone Center. Its modern architecture is a sight to behold and will surely catch your eye. Snap a few pictures and appreciate the sleek design before you step inside.

But wait, the real magic happens when you attend an event at Moscone Center. Whether it's a trade show, conference, concert, or any other happening, you'll find yourself in the midst of the action. Get ready to be surrounded by enthusiastic crowds, engaging exhibitions, and a vibrant atmosphere that will leave you buzzing with excitement.

From industry expos showcasing the latest innovations to cultural events celebrating art and entertainment, Moscone Center hosts a wide variety of gatherings that cater to different interests. It's an opportunity to learn, network, and have a great time all in one place.

While you're in town, make sure to take a look at the schedule of events happening at Moscone Center. This incredible venue is known for hosting iconic gatherings like Comic Con and FanExpo. You never know what amazing pop culture extravaganza or fan-filled convention you might stumble upon!

But even if there are no public events happening during your visit, fear not! The surrounding area is teeming with fantastic dining and nightlife options. So when you're done exploring the wonders of Moscone Center, you can head out to discover the vibrant culinary scene and lively bars nearby.

- Sightglass Coffee

Calling all coffee lovers! When you're in San Francisco, make sure to immerse yourself in the vibrant coffee culture that the city is famous for. And if you're looking for a truly iconic coffee experience, look no further than Sightglass Coffee.

While Sightglass Coffee has multiple locations throughout the city, you'll find one nestled in the heart of SoMa on 7th Street. But let me tell you, this is not your average coffee shop. It's a destination in itself, where the art of coffee takes center stage.

Step inside and you'll be greeted by the sight (pun intended!) of live coffee roasting. That's right, you can witness the magic of coffee beans being expertly roasted right before your eyes. The rustic, factory-style interiors give the place a unique and captivating ambiance that will transport you into the world of coffee craftsmanship.

But let's not forget the main event—the coffee itself. At Sightglass Coffee, they take their brews seriously. Every sip is an exquisite and refined experience, crafted with precision and passion. Whether you're a fan of espresso, pour-over, or something in between, their expertly brewed coffee will leave your taste buds dancing with delight.

And what pairs perfectly with a delicious cup of coffee? Delectable pastries, of course! Sightglass Coffee doesn't just excel in the art of coffee-making; they also know how to satisfy your sweet tooth. Indulge in their scrumptious pastries that complement the flavors of their coffee perfectly.

Orpheum Theater

Get ready to be swept away by the magic of theater at the magnificent Orpheum Theater! This stunning architectural gem, dating back to 1926, is a must-see for theater enthusiasts and architecture aficionados alike.

Located along Market Street, the Orpheum Theater stands as a testament to grandeur and elegance. From the moment you lay eyes on its ornate facade, you'll be transported to a bygone era of opulence and artistry.

But it's not just the breathtaking architecture that makes the Orpheum Theater a standout attraction. Prepare to be dazzled by the incredible plays that grace its stage. This iconic theater is home to some of the most renowned and beloved productions, including the unforgettable Hamilton and the enchanting Moulin Rouge.

Immerse yourself in the world of theater as the curtain rises and the performers transport you to captivating stories and breathtaking performances. From the powerful music of Hamilton to the dazzling spectacle of Moulin Rouge, each production at the Orpheum Theater promises an unforgettable experience that will leave you in awe.

- Charmaine's Rooftop Bar and Lounge

If you're searching for a cozy spot to spend quality time with your sweetheart, look no further than Charmaine's Rooftop Bar and Lounge. This place is pure romance, my friend!

Step into a world of enchantment as you soak in the intimate ambiance and delightful vibes. Prepare to be amazed by the breathtaking skyline views of San Francisco. Take it all in from their rooftop outdoor seating, especially at night when the city's shimmering skyscrapers come alive under the starry sky. It's pure magic!

Oh, and let's not forget about those stunning sunsets. Even if you choose to visit earlier in the day, you'll still be treated to a spectacle of colors that will take your breath away.

Now, I know what you're thinking—it can get chilly up there. But fear not! Charmaine's has got you covered with their gas-lit fire pits. Picture snuggling up with your loved one by the warm, flickering flames, creating an ambiance that's both cozy and serene. It's like a scene from a movie!

You'll find Charmaine's Rooftop Bar and Lounge nestled along the captivating streets of Market and McAllister.

- Rincon Park

Make sure to include a visit to Rincon Park in your SoMa itinerary. This delightful park offers the perfect opportunity to admire the beauty of the San Francisco Bay and take in the iconic San Francisco-Oakland Bay Bridge.

Located just a quick 5-minute drive from Salesforce Park, Rincon Park is a must-see destination for nature lovers and bridge enthusiasts alike. You can stroll along the park's scenic pathways, breathe in the fresh bay air, and soak up the breathtaking views of the water and the majestic bridge.

Take a leisurely walk along the waterfront, find a cozy spot to sit and relax, or even have a delightful picnic with your loved ones. The park provides a serene escape from the bustling city, allowing you to unwind and appreciate the natural beauty that surrounds you.

Don't forget your camera! Rincon Park offers plenty of Instagram-worthy moments, with the stunning bridge as your backdrop. Capture the perfect shot to remember your visit and share the beauty of San Francisco with friends and family.

Rincon Park is hands down the best spot to capture the grandeur of the San Francisco-Oakland Bay Bridge, one of the city's iconic landmarks.

As you stand in awe of this massive bridge, you'll appreciate the impressive feat of engineering that connects San Francisco to Oakland. The Bay Bridge, along with its counterpart, the world-famous Golden Gate Bridge, represents the remarkable infrastructure of the city.

Don't forget to check out the larger-than-life attraction at Rincon Park: **Cupid's Span**! This whimsical art installation will capture your attention with its giant bow and arrow, creating a playful and eye-catching landmark that has become synonymous with the park.

Rincon Park offers more than just a photo opportunity with Cupid's Span. It's the perfect place to take a leisurely stroll and soak in the refreshing San Francisco breezes. Whether you're enjoying a romantic walk with your partner or simply taking a moment to relax and unwind, Rincon Park provides a serene and picturesque setting to escape the hustle and bustle of the city.

- Oracle Park

Get ready for some sports action at Oracle Park, the ultimate destination for baseball fans and enthusiasts! Located just a stone's throw away from SoMa at Willie Mays Plaza, this iconic stadium is home to the legendary San Francisco Giants of Major League Baseball (MLB).

Step into the vibrant atmosphere of Oracle Park and immerse yourself in the thrilling world of America's favorite pastime.

Whether you're a die-hard baseball fan or simply want to experience the electric energy of a live sporting event, Oracle Park is an unmissable destination during your visit to SoMa.

As you enter the stadium, you'll be greeted by the impressive interior, ready to witness the heart-pounding action unfold on the field. Cheer on the Giants and be a part of the passionate crowd, creating an unforgettable atmosphere that embodies the rich sports culture of San Francisco.

But it doesn't end with baseball. Oracle Park offers more than just thrilling games. Surrounding the stadium, you'll find a plethora of restaurants and eateries to satisfy your cravings. Grab a bite to eat and soak in the beautiful views of Mission Bay, creating the perfect backdrop for a memorable day at the ballpark.

- Chase Center

Speaking of sports arenas, don't forget about Chase Center, another iconic destination near SoMa. Located in the vibrant Mission Bay area, this modern arena is home to the Golden State Warriors of the National Basketball Association (NBA).

Basketball fans will feel right at home as they witness the Warriors' dominance and celebrate their global success.

Chase Center isn't just for basketball games, though. It also hosts various concerts throughout the year, adding even more excitement to your visit. Check the schedule to see if there's a show that piques your interest during your stay.

Opened in 2019, Chase Center is a state-of-the-art sports arena that promises an unforgettable experience. With its modern facilities and electrifying atmosphere, it's a must-visit destination for sports enthusiasts and music lovers alike.

# CHAPTER FIVE

## Eating and Drinking

Best Restaurants in San Francisco

- Gary Danko

Gary Danko is a fancy restaurant near Fisherman's Wharf that offers an incredible dining experience. You can easily walk to Pier 39 and Ghirardelli Square from here.

You absolutely have to try their famous Roast Maine Lobster. When you take your first bite, the succulent lobster meat just melts in your mouth, and the rich sauce enhances the flavors perfectly. It comes with buttery mashed potatoes and seasonal vegetables that add an extra touch of deliciousness. Trust me, every bite is pure culinary bliss!

**Pros**: Impeccable service, an extensive wine list, and a menu that changes with the seasons to showcase the freshest ingredients.

**Cons**: It can be quite pricey, so it's best for special occasions or when you're feeling extra indulgent.

- State Bird Provisions

State Bird Provisions is a hip and innovative restaurant in the Western Addition neighborhood. It's near the famous Alamo Square Park, where you can enjoy breathtaking views of the Painted Ladies.

One dish that stands out at State Bird Provisions is their State Bird with Provisions. With each mouthwatering bite, you'll experience the tender and juicy quail paired with bold and flavorful sauces. The presentation is stunning, and the combination of textures and flavors will leave you wanting more.

**Pros**: Creative small plates served in a dim sum style, a lively and energetic atmosphere, and a menu that reflects the diverse culinary influences of San Francisco.

**Cons**: They don't take reservations, so be prepared to wait, especially during busy times.

- Zuni Café

Zuni Café is a beloved institution in the Civic Center neighborhood. Since 1979, they've been serving up delicious dishes to locals and visitors. You'll find it conveniently located near the San Francisco City Hall and the Asian Art Museum.

Their Zuni Roast Chicken is legendary. As you dig into the perfectly roasted chicken, you'll experience the crispy and golden skin revealing tender and juicy meat. The warm bread salad that accompanies it soaks up the flavorful pan drippings, creating a mouthwatering combination of tastes and textures.

**Pros**: Rustic and inviting atmosphere, a menu that celebrates local and seasonal ingredients, and an extensive wine list.

**Cons**: It can get busy, so making a reservation is recommended, especially for dinner.

- Burma Superstar

Burma Superstar is located in the Inner Richmond neighborhood, and it offers a culinary journey through Burmese cuisine. It's a great spot to visit after exploring Golden Gate Park.

The Tea Leaf Salad is a must-try at Burma Superstar. Each bite is a symphony of flavors and textures, with fermented tea leaves, crunchy nuts, and crispy garlic coming together in a delightful harmony. The sweet, savory, and tangy notes will dance on your palate and leave you craving more.

**Pros**: Flavorful and authentic Burmese cuisine, friendly and attentive service, and a welcoming and casual atmosphere.

**Cons**: It can get crowded, so expect a wait, especially during peak hours. Consider visiting during off-peak times to avoid the crowds.

- La Taqueria

La Taqueria is a popular spot in the Mission District for authentic Mexican street food. After your meal, head over to Dolores Park, which is nearby, and enjoy the sunshine.

When you're at La Taqueria, you have to try their signature Carne Asada Taco. The tender and flavorful grilled steak, nestled in a fresh handmade tortilla and topped with onions, cilantro, and salsa, is a flavor explosion in every bite. The perfectly seasoned meat, charred edges, and zingy salsa create a true fiesta of flavors that will transport you straight to Mexico.

**Pros**: Authentic and delicious Mexican street food, affordable prices, and a casual and lively atmosphere.

**Cons**: It can get crowded, so be prepared for a potential wait, especially during peak hours. The restaurant has limited seating, mainly counter-style dining.

## Local Cuisine and Specialties

**Local Cuisine in San Francisco:**

- Cioppino

As you take a spoonful of the hearty Cioppino, the aroma of the ocean envelops your senses. The rich tomato-based broth bursts with flavors of fresh seafood, from succulent Dungeness crab legs to tender shrimp, clams, and mussels. Each bite is a symphony of the sea, with hints of garlic, herbs, and a touch of spice. The crusty sourdough bread on the side soaks up the luscious broth, creating a perfect harmony of textures and tastes.

For the best Cioppino experience, head to Fisherman's Wharf, where you can find renowned seafood restaurants like Sotto Mare and Tadich Grill. These establishments serve up steaming bowls of Cioppino that will transport you straight to the shores of the Bay. Each spoonful is a harmonious blend of fresh seafood, tangy tomato broth, and aromatic herbs. Don't forget to grab a side of sourdough bread to soak up every last drop of that delectable goodness!

- Mission Burrito

Unwrap the Mission Burrito, and you'll be greeted by layers of warm tortilla embracing a delightful blend of seasoned grilled meat, rice, beans, cheese, salsa, and guacamole. With each bite, the tender meat, creamy beans, and tangy salsa dance on your palate, creating a burst of Mexican flavors. The generous portion and perfectly balanced ingredients make it a satisfying and comforting meal that captures the essence of San Francisco's vibrant Mission District.

For a taste of the Mission District's culinary treasures, head to La Taqueria or El Farolito, where you can indulge in the legendary Mission Burrito. These iconic taquerias craft burritos that are the stuff of legends.

- Dungeness Crab

Crack open the shell of a freshly steamed Dungeness Crab, and you'll discover a treasure trove of sweet, delicate meat. Each succulent bite transports you to the rugged coastlines of Northern California, where the crab was harvested. The natural sweetness is enhanced by a touch of butter, lemon, or a spicy dipping sauce. Savory and indulgent, Dungeness Crab is a true San Francisco delicacy that showcases the city's love for seafood. Head to places like Swan Oyster Depot or the Crab House at Pier 39 for a crab feast you won't forget.

- Sourdough Bread

Tear off a piece of warm, crusty San Francisco Sourdough Bread, and the tangy aroma fills the air. The crust crackles under your teeth, revealing a soft and chewy interior. The distinct tanginess dances on your taste buds, a result of the long fermentation process. Whether you enjoy it plain, with a slather of butter, or as the base for a sandwich, this iconic bread is a testament to the city's baking traditions and captures the essence of San Francisco's culinary heritage.

To get your hands on the best San Francisco Sourdough Bread, visit Boudin Bakery, a local institution that has been perfecting its sourdough recipe since 1849.

- It's-It Ice Cream Sandwich

Sink your teeth into an It's-It Ice Cream Sandwich, and you'll experience a nostalgic delight. The creamy vanilla ice cream is perfectly sandwiched between two old-fashioned oatmeal cookies, which are then dipped in rich, velvety chocolate. With each bite, the cold, smooth ice cream contrasts with the chewy cookies and the bittersweet chocolate coating, creating a satisfying blend of textures and flavors. The It's-It Ice Cream Sandwich is a timeless treat that has delighted San Francisco locals for generations. These scrumptious ice cream sandwiches can be found at various locations, including the It's-It Factory in Burlingame.

**Specialties in San Francisco:**

- Irish Coffee

Take a sip of the famous Irish Coffee, and you'll be transported to the cozy ambiance of an Irish pub. The hot coffee is infused with a generous pour of Irish whiskey, subtly sweetened with brown sugar, and topped with a fluffy layer of whipped cream. The first sip warms your soul as the robust coffee flavor blends harmoniously with the smooth warmth of the whiskey. The velvety whipped cream adds a touch of indulgence, making this classic San Francisco specialty a comforting and invigorating beverage.

For the best rendition of this classic drink, head to The Buena Vista Cafe, located near Fisherman's Wharf.

- Ghirardelli Chocolate

Indulge in a piece of Ghirardelli Chocolate, and your taste buds are greeted by velvety smoothness and rich cocoa flavors. Each bite reveals layers of complexity, from the deep notes of dark chocolate to the creamy sweetness of milk chocolate. The chocolate melts luxuriously on your tongue, releasing a symphony of flavors that reflect the craftsmanship and dedication of San Francisco's iconic chocolate brand. Ghirardelli Chocolate is a decadent treat that satisfies even the most discerning chocolate lover.

Get ready for a chocolatey adventure by visiting Ghirardelli Square, where you'll find the Ghirardelli Chocolate Company's flagship location.


- Sourdough Bread Bowl with Clam Chowder

As you break through the crisp crust of the Sourdough Bread Bowl, a delightful aroma of freshly baked bread fills the air. Inside, a steaming bowl of creamy Clam Chowder awaits. The thick soup is laden with tender clams, chunks of potatoes, and aromatic herbs. With each spoonful, the creamy broth envelops your taste buds, while the chunks of clam provide a burst of briny flavor. The sourdough bread, soaked in the savory soup, adds a delightful tang and a satisfying chew. This iconic San Francisco specialty is a comforting and hearty delight, perfect for cool coastal evenings.

For a taste of San Francisco's coastal flavors, head to Boudin Bakery, located in Fisherman's Wharf. Order their famous Sourdough Bread Bowl filled with hearty Clam Chowder, and prepare for a satisfying treat.

- Irish Soda Bread

Tear off a piece of warm, dense Irish Soda Bread, and you'll be greeted by the aroma of freshly baked goodness. The bread is slightly sweet with a subtle hint of nuttiness, thanks to the addition of raisins and caraway seeds. Its crumbly yet moist texture is a testament to the traditional baking techniques. As you take a bite, the bread melts in your mouth, releasing a delightful medley of flavors. Whether enjoyed plain, slathered with butter, or accompanied by a hearty Irish stew, Irish Soda Bread brings a taste of Ireland to the vibrant streets of San Francisco.

To savor the warmth and comfort of Irish Soda Bread in San Francisco, visit The Irish Bank, a lively pub located in the Financial District.

- Anchor Steam Beer

Raise a glass of refreshing Anchor Steam Beer and savor the essence of San Francisco's brewing history. As the golden amber liquid touches your lips, a symphony of caramel and toffee notes dances on your tongue. The smooth and crisp texture enhances the flavors, with a perfect balance of malty sweetness and a subtle hoppy bitterness. The distinctive yeast strain used in brewing gives Anchor Steam Beer its unique character and a hint of fruitiness. This iconic local brew is a tribute to San Francisco's rich beer heritage and a delightful libation to enjoy on a sunny afternoon or alongside a delectable meal.

For an authentic experience, head to Anchor Brewing Company in Potrero Hill.

## Food Trucks and Street Food

**Food Trucks**

- The Chairman

This popular food truck specializes in Asian-inspired street food with a modern twist. One of their signature dishes is the "Chairman Bao," a fluffy steamed bun filled with tender and flavorful braised pork belly, pickled daikon, and a touch of cilantro. The combination of soft and savory flavors makes it a must-try. Look out for The Chairman food truck in various locations throughout the city.

- Senor Sisig

If you're craving a fusion of Filipino and Mexican cuisine, Senor Sisig is the place to go. Their famous Sisig Burrito combines traditional Filipino Sisig, made with sizzling chopped pork, onions, and citrus flavors, with the convenience of a burrito. The tender meat, tangy sauce, and perfectly paired ingredients create a delightful explosion of flavors. Keep an eye out for Senor Sisig food trucks roaming around San Francisco.

- Curry Up Now

This food truck brings the vibrant flavors of Indian street food to the streets of San Francisco. One of their standout dishes is the "Sexy Fries," a delectable fusion of masala fries topped with a medley of chutneys, cheese, and onions. Each bite offers a delightful mix of textures and spices, making it a favorite among locals. Look for Curry Up Now food trucks at various locations for a satisfying Indian street food experience.

- The Creme Brulee Cart

If you have a sweet tooth, don't miss out on The Creme Brulee Cart. This dessert-focused food truck serves up creamy and perfectly torched creme brulee in a variety of flavors. Imagine cracking through the caramelized sugar crust to reveal a silky smooth custard with flavors like classic vanilla, chocolate, or even exotic options like lavender. Follow The Creme Brulee Cart on social media to catch them at different spots throughout the city.

- The RoliRoti Gourmet Rotisserie

This food truck is famous for its mouthwatering rotisserie chicken and porchetta. One of their standout offerings is the "RoliRoti Porchetta Sandwich." Picture succulent, slow-roasted pork seasoned with fragrant herbs and spices, served on a crispy roll with optional condiments like caramelized onions or arugula. The combination of tender meat, crispy skin, and flavorful toppings creates a satisfying and memorable sandwich. Find The RoliRoti Gourmet Rotisserie food truck at various locations for a taste of their delicious rotisserie creations.

**Street Food in San Francisco:**

- Hot Dogs

San Francisco is home to various street vendors offering classic American hot dogs. Try a hot dog topped with onions, mustard, and sauerkraut for a quintessential street food experience. Look for hot dog carts near popular attractions or in bustling areas like Union Square.

- Tacos

San Francisco's streets come alive with the enticing aroma of freshly made tacos. From traditional Mexican taquerias to modern fusion options, you'll find a variety of flavors and fillings to satisfy your taco cravings. Head to the Mission District for a wide selection of taquerias offering authentic street-style tacos.

- Dim Sum

Chinatown is the go-to destination for delicious and affordable dim sum. Stroll through the bustling streets and visit small shops and bakeries offering an array of steamed dumplings, buns, and savory treats. Grab a few different items, like pork buns or shrimp dumplings, and enjoy a flavor-packed dim sum feast.

- Ice Cream

On warm days, keep an eye out for ice cream trucks or carts serving up frozen treats. Indulge in classic flavors like vanilla, chocolate, or strawberry, or try unique and creative options like lavender, matcha, or salted caramel. You can find ice cream vendors near popular attractions like Fisherman's Wharf or in parks like Dolores Park, offering a refreshing and delightful street dessert.

- Churros

Crispy, golden churros dusted with cinnamon and sugar are a beloved street food in San Francisco. Look for churro stands or carts in busy areas like the Ferry Building Marketplace or outside popular events and festivals. Sink your teeth into a warm churro and enjoy the satisfying combination of crispy exterior and soft, doughy interior. Some vendors even offer filled churros with decadent fillings like chocolate or caramel.

Remember to follow local recommendations and check vendor locations and hours in advance to ensure the best street food experience. Enjoy exploring the vibrant and diverse street food scene in San Francisco!

## Best Bars and Nightlife Spots

**Best Bars in San Francisco:**

- Smuggler's Cove

Located in the Hayes Valley neighborhood, Smuggler's Cove is a tropical-themed tiki bar that offers an immersive experience. Highlights include an extensive rum selection, expertly crafted cocktails served in unique vessels, and a lively atmosphere.

**Pros**: Authentic tiki bar experience, knowledgeable bartenders, and a wide range of rum-based drinks.
**Cons**: Can get crowded, especially on weekends.

- Bourbon & Branch

Tucked away in the Tenderloin district, Bourbon & Branch is a hidden speakeasy-style bar known for its classic cocktails and atmospheric setting. Highlights include a secret entrance, reservation-only access to certain areas, and a menu featuring timeless libations.
**Pros**: Intimate and exclusive ambiance, skilled mixologists, and attention to detail.
**Cons**: Limited walk-in availability, strict house rules.

- Trick Dog

Located in the Mission District, Trick Dog is a popular neighborhood bar known for its creative and ever-changing cocktail menu. Highlights include artistic and themed menus, a vibrant and energetic atmosphere, and a rooftop patio.

**Pros**: Inventive cocktails, lively and approachable vibe, and a diverse crowd.

**Cons**: Limited seating, can get noisy during peak hours.

- The Alembic

Situated in the Haight-Ashbury neighborhood, The Alembic is a cozy and stylish bar that focuses on craft cocktails and a curated selection of spirits. Highlights include a rotating menu featuring seasonal ingredients, a knowledgeable bar staff, and a relaxed yet sophisticated ambiance.

**Pros**: High-quality cocktails, excellent whiskey selection, and a comfortable setting.

**Cons**: Limited seating, can get busy on weekends.

- Tommy's Joynt

Located near Van Ness Avenue, Tommy's Joynt is a historic and lively bar that embodies the spirit of San Francisco. Highlights include a vast selection of beers and spirits, hearty comfort food, and a festive and casual atmosphere.

**Pros**: Relaxed and welcoming vibe, affordable drinks, and live music on certain nights.

**Cons**: Can get crowded during peak hours, limited vegetarian/vegan options.

**Best Nightlife Spots in San Francisco:**

- DNA Lounge

A legendary nightlife venue in SoMa, DNA Lounge hosts a variety of events, including live music, DJ sets, and themed parties. Highlights include multiple stages, a diverse range of performances, and a vibrant and energetic atmosphere.

**Pros**: Eclectic programming, late-night hours, and a spacious layout.

**Cons**: Cover charges may apply, some events can get crowded.

- Temple Nightclub

Situated in SoMa, Temple Nightclub is a premier destination for electronic dance music enthusiasts. Highlights include state-of-the-art sound and lighting systems, renowned DJs, and a spacious dance floor.

**Pros**: Cutting-edge music experiences, VIP bottle service, and themed events.

**Cons**: Can be expensive, long lines on busy nights.

- Mezzanine

Located in SoMa, Mezzanine is a versatile venue known for hosting live music performances, DJ sets, and private events. Highlights include a large dance floor, top-notch sound system, and an industrial-chic atmosphere.

**Pros**: Eclectic lineup of events, spacious layout, and friendly staff.

**Cons**: Limited seating, cover charges for some events.

- The Stud

A historic LGBTQ+ nightclub in the South of Market district, The Stud offers a welcoming and inclusive environment for diverse communities. Highlights include drag shows, themed parties, and a sense of community.

**Pros**: LGBTQ+ nightlife landmark, diverse programming, and friendly atmosphere.

**Cons**: Limited capacity, cover charges may apply.

- Audio Nightclub

Situated in the heart of the trendy Mid-Market area, Audio Nightclub is a popular destination for electronic music lovers. Highlights include a top-of-the-line sound system, cutting-edge DJ performances, and a sleek and modern interior.

**Pros**: Stellar sound quality, intimate dance floor, and an underground atmosphere.

**Cons**: Limited seating, can get crowded on peak nights.

- The Fillmore

A historic music venue in the Western Addition neighborhood, The Fillmore is renowned for its rich musical legacy and intimate setting. Highlights include a diverse lineup of live performances spanning various genres, legendary acts, and a vibrant atmosphere. Pros: Iconic music venue, excellent acoustics, and a sense of music history. Cons: Limited seating, tickets may sell out quickly for popular shows.

- El Rio

Nestled in the Mission District, El Rio is a beloved neighborhood bar with a lively and inclusive atmosphere. Highlights include a spacious outdoor patio, live music, and various theme nights. Pros: Relaxed and unpretentious vibe, diverse crowd, and strong community spirit. Cons: Limited indoor seating, can get crowded during peak hours.

- Monarch

Located in the SoMa neighborhood, Monarch is a chic and upscale nightlife spot offering a blend of music, cocktails, and art. Highlights include a multi-level venue with different rooms, a rooftop garden, and a sophisticated ambiance. Pros: Stylish setting, diverse music genres, and a well-curated cocktail menu. Cons: Can be pricey, dress code enforced on certain nights.

- Raven Bar

Situated in the trendy South of Market district, Raven Bar is a sleek and stylish cocktail lounge known for its craft drinks and sophisticated atmosphere. Highlights include a curated selection of spirits, creative mixology, and an intimate setting. Pros: Upscale cocktail experience, attentive bartenders, and a refined ambiance. Cons: Limited seating, can get crowded on weekends.

- The View Lounge

Located atop the Marriott Marquis hotel, The View Lounge offers stunning panoramic views of the city skyline. Highlights include floor-to-ceiling windows, handcrafted cocktails, and a relaxed yet upscale ambiance. Pros: Unparalleled city views, comfortable seating, and a great spot for special occasions. Cons: Can be crowded during peak hours, drinks can be pricey due to the location.

Remember to check each establishment's website or call ahead to confirm their operating hours, entry requirements, and any COVID-19-related restrictions that may be in place. Enjoy exploring the vibrant nightlife scene in San Francisco!

# CHAPTER SIX

## Accommodation

### Best Hotels and Resorts

**Hotels**:

- The Ritz-Carlton, San Francisco.

Located in Nob Hill, The Ritz-Carlton offers luxurious accommodations with impeccable service.

**Pros**: Elegant rooms, a world-class spa, and a central location near Union Square.

**Cons**: Higher price range, limited on-site dining options.

- Hotel Drisco

Situated in Pacific Heights, Hotel Drisco is known for its classic charm and stunning views of the city.

**Pros**: Beautifully appointed rooms, complimentary breakfast and evening wine reception, and a quiet neighborhood setting.

**Cons**: A bit removed from the downtown area, limited dining options within walking distance.

- Fairmont San Francisco

Perched atop Nob Hill, the Fairmont San Francisco is an iconic hotel with grand architecture and a rich history.

**Pros**: Opulent rooms, a rooftop garden with panoramic views, and close proximity to Chinatown and Union Square.

**Cons**: Can be expensive, additional fees for amenities.

- Hotel Zephyr

Located in Fisherman's Wharf, Hotel Zephyr offers a playful and nautical-themed experience.

**Pros**: Funky and modern rooms, an outdoor lounge with fire pits, and close to popular attractions like Pier 39 and Ghirardelli Square.

**Cons**: Can get busy with tourists, limited dining options on-site.

- The St. Regis San Francisco

Situated in the vibrant SoMa neighborhood, The St. Regis exudes sophistication and contemporary luxury.

**Pros**: Stylish and spacious rooms, an indulgent spa, and easy access to the Museum of Modern Art and Yerba Buena Gardens.

**Cons**: High-end pricing, additional fees for certain amenities.

**Resorts**:

- Cavallo Point Lodge

Located in the Golden Gate National Recreation Area, Cavallo Point offers a serene retreat with breathtaking views of the Golden Gate Bridge.

**Pros**: Charming and rustic accommodations, a spa and wellness center, and proximity to hiking trails.

Cons: A bit secluded from the city center, limited dining options nearby.

- The Clift Royal Sonesta Hotel

Situated in Union Square, The Clift combines modern design with timeless elegance.

Pros: Artistic and unique rooms, a renowned Redwood Room bar, and easy access to shopping and dining in Union Square.

Cons: Can be noisy due to the central location, smaller room sizes.

- Argonaut Hotel

Located in Fisherman's Wharf, the Argonaut is a boutique hotel housed in a historic waterfront building.

Pros: Nautically-themed rooms, a lively atmosphere, and close proximity to popular attractions like Pier 39 and Alcatraz Landing.

Cons: Can be busy with tourists, limited on-site amenities.

- The Lodge at the Presidio

Situated within the Presidio National Park, The Lodge offers a tranquil and nature-filled escape.

**Pros**: Historic and beautifully restored rooms, stunning views of the park, and access to hiking trails and outdoor activities.

**Cons**: A bit removed from downtown, limited dining options within walking distance.

- The Stanyan Park Hotel

Located near Golden Gate Park, The Stanyan Park Hotel is a charming and historic property.

**Pros**: Victorian-style rooms, a cozy and inviting atmosphere, and close proximity to Golden Gate Park and Haight-Ashbury.

**Cons**: Not as centrally located, limited on-site amenities.

## Hostels and Budget Lodging

**Hostels**:

- HI San Francisco Downtown

Located in the heart of the city near Union Square, HI San Francisco Downtown offers budget-friendly accommodations with a social atmosphere.

**Pros**: Central location, organized activities and events, and a communal kitchen.

**Cons**: Shared facilities, limited privacy.

- Green Tortoise Hostel

Situated in the North Beach neighborhood, the Green Tortoise Hostel provides a lively and social experience for travelers.

**Pros**: Fun and friendly atmosphere, free breakfast and dinners, and close proximity to popular attractions like Chinatown and Fisherman's Wharf.

**Cons**: Shared facilities, noise can be an issue.

- Pacific Tradewinds Hostel

Situated in the Financial District, Pacific Tradewinds Hostel provides a cozy and welcoming environment for budget-conscious travelers.

**Pros**: Friendly and helpful staff, organized group outings, and proximity to the Embarcadero and Ferry Building.

**Cons**: Limited common space, shared facilities.

- Adelaide Hostel

Located in the lively Union Square area, Adelaide Hostel offers affordable accommodations in a historic building.

**Pros**: Great value for the price, complimentary breakfast, and a convenient location for shopping and dining.

**Cons**: Shared facilities, can be noisy due to the central location.

**Budget Lodging:**
- Civic Center Motor Inn

Situated near the Civic Center neighborhood, Civic Center Motor Inn provides comfortable and budget-friendly rooms for travelers.

**Pros**: Free parking, spacious rooms, and easy access to public transportation.

**Cons**: Basic amenities, not as centrally located.

- Motel Capri

Located in the Marina District, Motel Capri offers affordable accommodations in a convenient and trendy neighborhood.

**Pros**: Free parking, clean and comfortable rooms, and proximity to Marina Green and the Palace of Fine Arts.

**Cons**: Limited amenities, not within walking distance of major tourist attractions.

- The Mosser Hotel

Located near Union Square, The Mosser Hotel offers budget-friendly accommodations with a boutique atmosphere.

**Pros**: Unique and stylish rooms, complimentary Wi-Fi, and easy access to shopping and dining.

**Cons**: Shared bathroom facilities in some rooms, limited on-site amenities.

- European Hostel

Situated in the North Beach neighborhood, European Hostel provides budget lodging options in a vibrant area.

**Pros**: Affordable rates, convenient location for exploring Chinatown and Fisherman's Wharf, and a communal kitchen.

**Cons**: Shared facilities, noise can be an issue.

## Vacation Rentals and Apartments

**Vacation Rentals:**

- Airbnb

Airbnb offers a wide range of vacation rentals throughout San Francisco, allowing you to choose from various locations, sizes, and amenities.

**Pros**: Flexible options, potential for unique and personalized experiences, and the ability to connect with local hosts.

**Cons**: Varying quality and reliability, potential for additional fees.

- VRBO

VRBO (Vacation Rentals by Owner) provides a selection of vacation homes and apartments in San Francisco.

**Pros**: A diverse range of properties, often with more space and amenities than hotels, and the potential for cost savings for larger groups or longer stays.

**Cons**: Limited interaction with hosts, potential for less responsive customer service.

- HomeAway

HomeAway offers a variety of vacation rentals, including apartments, houses, and condos in San Francisco.

**Pros**: Wide selection of properties, often with full kitchens and other home-like amenities, and the potential for more privacy and space.

**Cons**: Booking process can be complex, potential for hidden fees.

- FlipKey

FlipKey, a TripAdvisor company, provides vacation rentals with a focus on quality and reliability.

**Pros**: Rigorous vetting process for properties, verified guest reviews, and a large inventory of options.

**Cons**: Limited availability compared to other platforms, potentially higher prices.

- Booking.com

While primarily known for hotels, Booking.com also offers vacation rentals in San Francisco.

**Pros**: Familiar and trusted platform, ability to compare options and prices, and access to customer support.

**Cons**: Fewer options compared to specialized vacation rental platforms, potential for higher fees.

**Apartments**:

- Avalon Dogpatch

Located in the Dogpatch neighborhood, Avalon Dogpatch offers modern apartments with amenities such as fitness centers and rooftop decks.

**Pros**: Contemporary living spaces, on-site amenities, and proximity to attractions like the Museum of the African Diaspora and AT&T Park.

**Cons**: Potentially higher rates, limited availability.

- NEMA

Situated in the Mid-Market district, NEMA provides upscale apartments with luxury amenities like a rooftop pool and fitness center.

**Pros**: High-end finishes and features, convenient location for exploring downtown San Francisco, and proximity to the San Francisco Museum of Modern Art.

**Cons**: Premium pricing, limited availability.

- Trinity Place

Located in the Civic Center neighborhood, Trinity Place offers a range of apartment options with amenities such as a fitness center and resident lounge.

**Pros**: Well-maintained apartments, central location near City Hall and the Asian Art Museum, and proximity to public transportation.

**Cons**: Potentially higher rents, limited parking availability.

- Venn on Market

Situated in the Castro district, Venn on Market provides contemporary apartments with amenities like a fitness center and rooftop lounge.

**Pros**: Stylish living spaces, vibrant neighborhood with LGBTQ+ history, and proximity to the Castro Theatre and local dining options.

**Cons**: Limited availability, potential for higher rents.

San Francisco is renowned for its diverse and vibrant culinary scene, with numerous restaurants offering a wide range of cuisines. Depending on the location of the vacation rental or apartment, you may find an array of dining options within walking distance or a short drive away. Popular areas for dining in San Francisco include the Mission District, Chinatown, North Beach, and the Embarcadero. Exploring these neighborhoods will allow you to discover local eateries, trendy cafes, and renowned dining establishments.

Remember to research and read reviews when choosing a vacation rental or apartment, as factors such as cleanliness, safety, and reliability can vary. It's also worth considering the amenities and facilities provided, such as laundry facilities, parking options, and kitchen equipment, depending on your specific needs.

# CHAPTER SEVEN

## Activities and Events

### Outdoor Activities

- Lands End Trail

This scenic coastal trail offers breathtaking views of the Pacific Ocean, Golden Gate Bridge, and rugged cliffs. It takes you through a mix of forested areas and open meadows, providing a great opportunity for birdwatching and exploring historic landmarks.

- Golden Gate Park

This expansive urban park offers a variety of outdoor activities. You can rent a bike and ride along the park's many trails, including the popular Panhandle and JFK Drive. Explore the park's gardens, lakes, and iconic landmarks like the Japanese Tea Garden and Conservatory of Flowers.

- Presidio Trails

The Presidio is a former military base turned national park with numerous hiking and biking trails. The Ecology Trail, Bay Area Ridge Trail, and Batteries to Bluffs Trail are all great options for outdoor enthusiasts. Enjoy stunning views of the Golden Gate Bridge and explore the park's diverse ecosystems.

- Mount Sutro Open Space Reserve

Located near the University of California, San Francisco, this hidden gem offers a network of trails through a dense eucalyptus forest. It's a peaceful retreat from the city, with winding paths and panoramic views of downtown San Francisco and the Bay.

- Marin Headlands

Just across the Golden Gate Bridge, the Marin Headlands offer a variety of hiking and biking trails with stunning coastal views. The Tennessee Valley Trail, Rodeo Valley Trail, and Coastal Trail are popular options. Don't miss the Point Bonita Lighthouse for a unique and picturesque experience.

## Festivals and Events

- San Francisco Pride Parade and Celebration

Held in late June, the San Francisco Pride Parade and Celebration is one of the largest LGBTQ+ pride events in the world. The parade winds through the streets of downtown, showcasing colorful floats, lively music, and vibrant costumes. The celebration continues at Civic Center Plaza with live performances, community booths, and a festive atmosphere promoting equality and inclusion.

- Outside Lands Music and Arts Festival

Taking place in Golden Gate Park in August, the Outside Lands Music and Arts Festival is a three-day extravaganza featuring an impressive lineup of renowned musicians, bands, and artists across various genres. Attendees can enjoy live music performances, interactive art installations, delicious food and drink offerings, and even comedy acts in a beautiful outdoor setting.

- San Francisco International Film Festival

As one of the longest-running film festivals in the Americas, the San Francisco International Film Festival attracts cinephiles from around the world. Held in April, the festival showcases a diverse range of films, including documentaries, narrative features, and experimental works. Screenings take place in various theaters throughout the city, accompanied by panel discussions, filmmaker Q&As, and special events.

- Hardly Strictly Bluegrass

This free music festival held in September in Golden Gate Park celebrates the rich tradition of bluegrass, folk, and Americana music. Hardly Strictly Bluegrass brings together renowned musicians and emerging artists for a weekend of performances across multiple stages. The festival's relaxed atmosphere and beautiful park setting make it a beloved event for music lovers of all ages.

- Carnaval San Francisco

Drawing inspiration from the Latin American and Caribbean carnival traditions, Carnaval San Francisco is a vibrant multicultural celebration held in the Mission District in May. The event features a grand parade filled with colorful floats, dancers in elaborate costumes, live music, and street performers. Additionally, there are food vendors offering delicious international cuisine and arts and crafts booths showcasing the diversity of the community.

# CHAPTER EIGHT

## Day Trips and Excursions

### Napa Valley

**Napa Valley Top Picks**

- Vineyards

Get ready for an incredible adventure in Napa Valley, where you'll discover picturesque vineyards and top-notch wineries. Visit renowned estates like Robert Mondavi Winery, Beringer Vineyards, and Domaine Chandon for tours, tastings, and fascinating insights into winemaking. Each winery has its own unique charm and offers the opportunity to sample exceptional wines.

- Wine Train

Hop aboard the Napa Valley Wine Train, a vintage rail experience that combines stunning views with gourmet dining. Relax on the train as it takes you through the breathtaking Napa Valley landscape while you indulge in a multi-course meal paired with local wines. It's the perfect way to unwind and soak in the beauty of the region.

- Castello di Amorosa

Don't miss the chance to explore Castello di Amorosa, a medieval-style castle and winery that's a must-visit attraction in Napa Valley. Take a captivating tour of the castle's grand halls, underground caves, and wine cellars. The castle's architecture and vineyard views make it a truly memorable experience.

- Balloon Ride

For a truly unique perspective, embark on a hot air balloon ride over Napa Valley. Float above the vineyards and be mesmerized by the breathtaking vistas of rolling hills, wineries, and the valley below. It's a magical way to kickstart your day trip and create unforgettable memories.

- Food Scene

Foodies, head to downtown Napa and immerse yourself in the culinary paradise of Oxbow Public Market. Explore the market's diverse stalls offering artisanal cheeses, fresh seafood, locally sourced produce, and gourmet chocolates. It's the perfect spot to grab a delicious bite, stock up on picnic supplies, or simply soak in the lively atmosphere.

To reach Napa Valley from San Francisco, it usually takes about 1.5 to 2 hours by car, depending on traffic and your destination. If you prefer public transportation, you can take the Napa Valley Vine Transit bus service from various San Francisco locations to Napa. Another option is to catch a ferry from San Francisco to Vallejo and then hop on a bus to Napa. Keep in mind that public transportation schedules may be limited and transfers might be required, so plan your trip accordingly.

Napa Valley's geography is characterized by rolling hills, lush vineyards, and charming towns. The region is divided into distinct appellations, each with its own microclimate and grape varieties, resulting in a rich diversity of wines.

When it comes to dining, Napa Valley offers a myriad of culinary experiences. Many wineries have their own restaurants or offer food pairings, allowing you to enjoy delicious meals alongside their wines. You'll also find numerous acclaimed restaurants, including Michelin-starred establishments, where you can savor gourmet cuisine featuring locally sourced ingredients.

Before embarking on your day trip to Napa Valley, remember to check the opening hours and availability of tours and tastings at the wineries you plan to visit. It's also a good idea to make reservations for dining experiences, especially during peak seasons, to ensure you have a spot at these popular establishments. Enjoy your trip and savor the beauty and flavors of Napa Valley.

## Silicon Valley

**Silicon Valley Top Picks**

- Computer History Museum

Ready to dive into the amazing world of computing? Head over to the Computer History Museum in Mountain View! You'll embark on a journey through the evolution of technology with interactive exhibits, cool artifacts, and captivating displays. It's a must-visit spot for all you tech enthusiasts who want to uncover the captivating history of computers and their impact on society.

- Stanford University

Picture yourself strolling through the gorgeous campus of Stanford University in Palo Alto. Prepare to be wowed by the stunning architecture, visit the incredible Cantor Arts Center, and bask in the peaceful atmosphere of the sprawling grounds. Oh, and don't forget to check out the awe-inspiring Stanford Memorial Church, a real architectural gem that will leave you breathless.

- The Tech Interactive

Calling all science and tech lovers! The Tech Interactive in San Jose is the place to be. This awesome museum lets you dive right into the world of science and technology with hands-on exhibits, mind-blowing virtual reality experiences, and educational programs that will blow your mind. Get ready to be inspired by cutting-edge innovations and explore the endless possibilities of the future.

- NASA Ames Visitor Center

Prepare to blast off into the exciting realm of space exploration at the NASA Ames Visitor Center in Mountain View. Get ready to learn all about NASA's mind-blowing research and mind-expanding discoveries. Marvel at the jaw-dropping spacecraft models and explore mind-boggling exhibits that showcase the wonders of space. And don't even get us started on the mind-blowing immersive theater presentations that will take you on an out-of-this-world journey.

- Apple Park Visitor Center

Calling all Apple aficionados! The Apple Park Visitor Center in Cupertino is your golden ticket to the headquarters of one of the coolest tech companies in the world. Get your hands on the latest Apple products and exclusive merchandise at the Apple Store. And make sure you check out the rooftop terrace for jaw-dropping panoramic views of the Apple Park campus and the surrounding area. It's an experience you won't want to miss!

Getting to Silicon Valley from San Francisco is a breeze! Just hop in a car, and you'll be there in 45 minutes to 1 hour (traffic depending, of course). If you prefer public transportation, catch the Caltrain from San Francisco to different stations in Silicon Valley. Once you arrive, you can hop on local buses or ride-sharing services to reach your desired destinations. Just remember to plan ahead, check schedules, and routes to make your trip smooth sailing.

Geographically, Silicon Valley sits pretty to the south of San Francisco and offers a unique blend of urban and suburban areas. You'll find an exciting mix of tech companies, research institutions, and vibrant communities. Get ready to explore modern office complexes, charming residential neighborhoods, and breathtaking landscapes all in one place.

Now let's talk about food, because Silicon Valley knows how to satisfy your taste buds! Whether you're into trendy cafes, mouthwatering food trucks, upscale restaurants, or exotic flavors, you'll find it all here. The culinary scene is diverse and caters to all tastes and dietary preferences, so get ready for innovative and healthy dishes that will make your taste buds dance with joy.

To make the most of your day trip to Silicon Valley, it's a smart move to plan your itinerary in advance. Make sure you allocate enough time for each attraction, and remember that some places might require advance reservations. So, check their websites or give them a call beforehand to avoid any disappointments. Get ready for an adventure in the world of technology and innovation. Silicon Valley awaits you with open arms.

## Muir Woods

**Muir Woods Top Picks**

- Muir Woods National Monument

Welcome to the incredible Muir Woods, a coastal redwood forest that will blow your mind! Get ready for an awe-inspiring adventure as you take a leisurely stroll along the well-kept trails. Brace yourself for the humbling experience of standing next to towering trees and soaking in the serene atmosphere. It's like stepping into a real-life fairytale!

- Cathedral Grove

Make sure you stop by Cathedral Grove, where you'll find the grandest and oldest redwoods in the entire forest. Prepare to be amazed by the majestic height of these ancient giants and take a moment to fully absorb the tranquility of this magical grove. It's a place where nature's beauty truly shines.

- Bohemian Grove Trail

Calling all hikers! The Bohemian Grove Trail is the perfect choice for a moderate adventure. Follow this path for a more secluded and peaceful experience, as it leads you deeper into the heart of the redwood forest. You'll feel like you're in a secret oasis of natural beauty.

- Fern Creek Trail

Want to immerse yourself in a picturesque journey through the woods? The Fern Creek Trail is your ticket! Get ready to be enchanted by babbling creeks, lush ferns, and the overall enchanting atmosphere. It's a trail that will transport you to a whole new world of beauty.

To reach Muir Woods from San Francisco, it's a scenic drive of around 30 minutes to 1 hour, depending on traffic and where you start. Get your camera ready as you cross the iconic Golden Gate Bridge and wind along roads that offer jaw-dropping views of the coastline and hills. It's a road trip you won't want to miss!

Geographically, Muir Woods is nestled in the coastal hills of Marin County, just north of San Francisco. Picture a hidden gem tucked away in a canyon alongside Redwood Creek, surrounded by lush vegetation and natural wonders. It's the kind of place that will make you feel like you've stepped into a different world.

When it's time to satisfy your hunger, remember that Muir Woods itself has limited food options. It's best to grab a bite before or after your visit. Don't worry, though! In nearby areas like Mill Valley or Sausalito, you'll find charming cafes, delightful restaurants, and tempting bakeries that will cater to your cravings. Treat yourself to some delicious eats and keep your energy levels up for the adventure ahead.

If you prefer to use public transportation to reach Muir Woods, here's a helpful tip. Catch a ferry from San Francisco to the picturesque waterfront town of

Sausalito. From there, hop on a local bus like the Marin Transit Route 61, which will whisk you away to Muir Woods. Remember to check the bus schedules in advance and plan your return trip accordingly to make your journey smooth sailing.

Another option is to combine public transportation and hiking for an extra adventure. Start by taking a ferry from San Francisco to Tiburon. Then, jump on the Marin Transit Route 219, which will drop you off near the Dipsea Trailhead. From there, follow the scenic Dipsea Trail all the way to Muir Woods. It's a fantastic way to experience both the wonders of public transportation and the beauty of nature.

Before you head out, remember to check the schedules and routes of public transportation options, as they can vary. To avoid crowds, it's also a good idea to arrive early, especially on weekends and holidays. If you want to be extra prepared, consider making advance reservations, especially during peak times, to secure your entry.

Get ready for an unforgettable day trip surrounded by the jaw-dropping beauty of Muir Woods. Let the tranquility wash over you, explore the enchanting trails, and

## Berkeley

Berkeley is a happening and diverse city that's perfect for a day trip full of exploration and fun! Check out these awesome places:

- UC Berkeley

Kick off your adventure by visiting the world-renowned University of California, Berkeley campus. Take a leisurely walk through Sproul Plaza, marvel at the stunning architecture, and feel the vibrant energy of this prestigious institution.

- Berkeley Marina

Head to the waterfront and soak in the stunning views at Berkeley Marina. Enjoy a leisurely stroll along the marina, try out kayaking or paddleboarding, or simply relax by the bay. And guess what? You can grab a delicious bite to eat at the marina's restaurants and cafes while you take in the scenery!

- Berkeley Art Museum and Pacific Film Archive

Art lovers, this one's for you! Don't miss the Berkeley Art Museum and Pacific Film Archive. Immerse yourself in a world of creativity and culture as you explore their amazing collection of art and film exhibits. From contemporary masterpieces to classic cinema, there's something to inspire everyone.

- Tilden Regional Park

Need some nature time? Make your way to Tilden Regional Park. This expansive park is a paradise for outdoor enthusiasts. With hiking trails, picnic spots, a botanical garden, and even a whimsical carousel, you'll have a blast! Oh, and don't forget to take a dip or unwind on the beach at the beautiful Lake Anza.

Getting to Berkeley from San Francisco usually takes around 30 minutes to an hour by car, depending on traffic and where you start. The distance between the two cities is roughly 13 miles (21 kilometers). As you drive, enjoy the scenic views on the Bay Bridge or the Richmond-San Rafael Bridge—it's like a mini-adventure within your day trip!

Geographically, Berkeley is nestled on the eastern shore of the San Francisco Bay, between Oakland and Albany. Its hilly terrain and diverse neighborhoods add to its unique charm. Expect a mix of urban vibes, residential areas, and pockets of natural beauty, making Berkeley a truly captivating place to explore.

Now, let's talk food! Berkeley is a foodie's dream come true. You'll discover an incredible range of dining options, from cozy cafes to fancy restaurants. The city is especially known for its culinary diversity and commitment to sustainable, locally sourced ingredients. Whatever your taste buds crave—international delights, vegetarian or vegan fare, or farm-to-table goodness—Berkeley has got you covered!

To navigate public transportation from San Francisco to Berkeley, here's what you need to know. BART (Bay Area Rapid Transit) is your friend. Hop on a BART train at stations like Embarcadero or Montgomery Street in San Francisco, and ride it to Downtown Berkeley Station. It's a quick journey of around 20-30 minutes, depending on the route you choose.

Another option is taking an AC Transit bus from San Francisco to Berkeley. Look out for bus lines like the F Line or the NL Line—they're your ticket to Berkeley fun!

Be sure to check the bus schedules and routes in advance, as they may vary throughout the day.

Once you're in Berkeley, hop on the local bus system, AC Transit, to effortlessly move around the city and reach all the cool attractions. With their extensive network of bus lines, getting from place to place will be a breeze.

Remember to check the schedules, plan your trip wisely, and consider having a transit map or using a navigation app to keep you on the right track.

Berkeley is calling, and it's ready to wow you with its vibrant culture, stunning parks, and mouthwatering food scene. Have a blast on your day trip, soak up the city's unique vibes, and create unforgettable memories in this lively destination.

## Oakland

Oakland, the city buzzing with energy and bursting with culture, is an absolute blast for a day trip. Get ready for some fantastic adventures at these must-see spots:

- Oakland Museum of California

Kick off your exploration at the Oakland Museum of California, where you can dive headfirst into the art, history, and natural wonders of the Golden State. It's a treasure trove of exhibits showcasing the diverse cultures and fascinating stories that make California so special.

- Lake Merritt

Get yourself to the heart of Oakland and discover the enchanting Lake Merritt. This urban oasis is surrounded by lively parks and bustling neighborhoods. Take a leisurely stroll, rent a kayak, or find a cozy spot for a picnic. The picturesque scenery will leave you feeling refreshed and rejuvenated.

- Jack London Square

Venture over to Jack London Square, an animated waterfront area named after the famous American author. Feel the lively vibes as you dine at waterfront restaurants, explore unique shops, and soak in the breathtaking views of the San Francisco Bay. Take a leisurely walk along the marina and let the bay breeze invigorate your spirit.

- Oakland Chinatown

Immerse yourself in the vibrant culture and mouth watering flavors of Oakland Chinatown. The bustling streets are lined with markets, shops, and authentic eateries waiting to be explored. Be sure to treat yourself to delicious dim sum, boba tea, or traditional Chinese pastries for an unforgettable culinary adventure.

- Redwood Regional Park

Need a nature fix? Look no further than Redwood Regional Park. This remarkable park offers serene redwood forests, picturesque trails, and idyllic picnic spots. Take a hike amidst towering trees, breathe in the crisp, fresh air, and let the tranquility of nature wash over you.

To get to Oakland from San Francisco, hop in a car and expect a journey of around 20-40 minutes, depending on traffic and where you start. The distance between the two cities is roughly 10 miles (16 kilometers). As you cross the Bay Bridge, marvel at the stunning views of the bay and the city skyline that will leave you in awe.

Geographically, Oakland is located on the eastern side of the San Francisco Bay, just east of San Francisco. It's a city with diverse neighborhoods, ranging from bustling downtown areas to charming residential hills. You'll find a captivating blend of urban landscapes, breathtaking waterfront views, and picturesque parks, making Oakland a place of delightful contrasts.

When it's time to refuel, Oakland's culinary scene won't disappoint. Prepare for a taste bud extravaganza! The city is brimming with options, from trendy eateries and gourmet restaurants to ethnic cuisines and mouth watering food trucks. Embrace the opportunity to sample the local specialties and embark on a culinary adventure you won't soon forget.

To navigate public transportation from San Francisco to Oakland, here are some handy tips. BART (Bay Area Rapid Transit) is a fantastic choice. Hop on a BART train at stations like Embarcadero or Montgomery Street in San Francisco, and let it whisk you away to downtown Oakland. The ride typically takes 15-20 minutes, depending on the route you take.

Another option is to hop on a ferry from San Francisco to Oakland. Enjoy a scenic journey across the bay and disembark at Jack London Square, a convenient hub for exploring the city.

Once you're in Oakland, you can rely on the local bus system, AC Transit, to zip around town and reach your desired attractions. With its extensive network of bus lines, getting around the city is a breeze.

Remember to check schedules, plan your itinerary wisely, and consider having a transit map or using a nifty navigation app to help you navigate the routes like a pro.

# CHAPTER NINE

## Practical Information

### Getting Around San Francisco

- **Public Transportation**:

**BART (Bay Area Rapid Transit):** BART is your speedy ticket to exploring San Francisco and its surroundings. Grab a Clipper card for sweet deals and easy transfers between BART and other modes of transport.

**Muni**: Muni's got you covered with buses, streetcars, and cable cars. Score a Muni Passport for unlimited rides and roam the city like a local. Don't forget to validate your ticket when you hop on a bus or streetcar.

Fares and Discounts: Score discounts for seniors, kids, and folks with disabilities. Daily, weekly, or monthly passes are wallet-friendly if you plan to ride public transport like a champ.

- **Cable Cars and Historic Streetcars:**

**Cable Cars:** Hop on San Francisco's famous cable cars and soak in the charm. Expect lines, especially at popular stops like Powell Street. Try riding during off-peak hours for a quicker trip.

**Historic Streetcars**: Ride back in time on the vintage streetcars along the F-Line. These restored beauties offer a nostalgic journey through the city's coolest neighborhoods and waterfront.

- **Bicycles and Scooters:**

**Bike Rentals**: Pedal power is the way to go! Rent a bike from one of SF's many shops and explore the city on two wheels. Ride across the Golden Gate Bridge for epic views all the way to Sausalito.

**Scooter Sharing**: Zoom around the city on electric scooters. Look out for Lime, Bird, or Spin for a thrilling ride. Remember to follow traffic rules and park those scooters responsibly.

- **Ride-Sharing and Taxis:**

**Ride-Sharing Apps:** Uber and Lyft are your trusty sidekicks in SF. Check prices and availability before booking. Shared rides can save you some dough if you're cool with sharing the adventure.

**Taxis**: Flag down a classic taxi or find one at designated stands. They're a reliable option, but fares might be higher than ride-sharing services.

- **Walking**:

San Francisco is made for strolling! With attractions within walking distance, put on comfy shoes, layer up, and be ready for the city's ever-changing weather.

Use a nifty navigation app to find the best routes, uncover hidden gems, and uncover local landmarks on foot.

- **Golden Gate Ferry**:

Take a scenic trip on the Golden Gate Ferry across the bay to Sausalito or Marin County. Marvel at the majestic Golden Gate Bridge and the stunning San Francisco skyline along the way.

- Tips for Getting the Best Deal:

**Clipper Card**: Snap up a Clipper card for discounted fares and smooth transfers across various transport systems.

**Visitor Passes**: Grab visitor passes like the CityPASS or Go San Francisco Card for bundled discounts on attractions and transport.

**Off-Peak Hours**: Travel during quieter times to avoid crowds and potential price surges for ride-sharing services.

**Check Fare Options**: Explore different fare choices like daily or multi-day passes to save some bucks if you're planning to ride public transport like a boss.

**Plan Ahead**: Research transport options, schedules, and routes beforehand to make the most of your adventure and dodge unnecessary waiting times.

## Safety Tips

Ready to explore the amazing city of San Francisco? Safety is key to a fantastic trip, so check out these tips for a fun and secure adventure:

**Keep an eye out**: Stay alert and aware of your surroundings, especially in busy areas and popular tourist spots. Keep your belongings close and be on the lookout for anything suspicious.

**Stick to the light:** Bright and bustling areas are your best bet, especially at night. Avoid dark streets or isolated spots that might not be as safe.

**Secure your stuff**: Keep your valuables, like wallets, phones, and cameras, secure and out of sight. Opt for a cross-body bag or a backpack and always keep it close. Watch out for sneaky pickpockets, especially in crowded places.

**Stay savvy on public transport**: San Francisco's public transportation is generally safe, but it doesn't hurt to stay cautious. Be aware of your surroundings and keep an eye on your belongings when riding buses, trains, or cable cars.

**Go with the pros**: When using ride-sharing services or taxis, go for reputable and licensed companies. Double-check the driver's info and make sure the license plate matches before hopping in.

**Stay street smart**: San Francisco has its fair share of street vendors, panhandlers, and solicitors. Use your judgment and be cautious if strangers approach you asking for money or offering unsolicited services.

**Dress to adapt**: San Francisco's weather can be unpredictable, with fog, wind, and temperature changes throughout the day. Layer up to adapt to the ever-changing conditions and make sure to wear comfy shoes for the city's hilly terrain.

**Plan like a pro**: Before setting off, plan your routes and do some research on the areas you'll be exploring. Stick to well-known tourist spots and neighborhoods, and be extra careful if venturing into unfamiliar or remote areas.

**Trust the experts:** If you need assistance or info, visit official tourist information centers or ask your hotel staff. They're there to provide reliable guidance and helpful advice.

**Trust your gut:** Your instincts are powerful, so listen to them. If something doesn't feel right or seems unsafe, trust your intuition and remove yourself from the situation. It's always better to be cautious than to take unnecessary risks.

## Money Matters

- Budget Travelers:

**Accommodation**: Look for affordable options like budget hotels, hostels, or vacation rentals in less touristy areas such as the Mission District or Tenderloin.

**Dining**: Save money by trying local food trucks, affordable eateries, or tasty ethnic restaurants throughout the city.

**Transportation**: Take advantage of public transportation like buses and trains, and grab a Clipper card for discounted fares. Walking or biking are also great, cost-effective ways to explore the city.

**Attractions**: Check out free or low-cost attractions like Golden Gate Park, walking across the Golden Gate Bridge, or visiting museums on specific days with free entry.

**Shopping**: Find unique treasures and good deals at local flea markets, thrift stores, or discounted outlets.

- Mid-Range Tourists:

**Accommodation**: Consider moderately priced hotels or boutique accommodations in popular areas like Union Square or Fisherman's Wharf. Look out for deals and discounts when booking.

**Dining**: Enjoy a mix of affordable and mid-range dining options. Dive into the city's diverse culinary scene without breaking the bank.

**Transportation**: Combine public transportation, ride-sharing services, and taxis for convenience. Plan your trips efficiently to save on transportation costs.

**Attractions**: Save money on admission fees with bundled attraction passes like the CityPASS or Go San

Francisco Card. Take guided tours or hop on a hop-off bus for a comprehensive city experience.

Shopping: Explore shopping districts like Union Square, Westfield San Francisco Centre, or Hayes Valley for a range of mid-range retail options.

- Luxury Travelers:

**Accommodation**: Spoil yourself with luxury hotels in prime areas like Nob Hill or Embarcadero. Look for amenities like spa services, rooftop bars, or breathtaking views.

**Dining**: Indulge in fine dining at Michelin-starred restaurants or upscale eateries known for their exceptional cuisine and ambiance. Don't miss out on San Francisco's renowned seafood and farm-to-table options.

**Transportation**: Enjoy the comfort and convenience of private car services or chauffeur-driven experiences. Consider hiring private guides for personalized city tours.

**Attractions**: Opt for exclusive experiences and VIP access to attractions like Alcatraz Island, private museum tours, or helicopter rides for a unique perspective of the city.

**Shopping**: Discover luxury shopping destinations like Union Square, Fillmore Street, or the Embarcadero, where you'll find high-end designer boutiques and upscale department stores.

No matter your budget, keep track of your expenses and consider travel insurance. Look for deals and discounts that suit your travel style, and allocate funds for souvenirs and unexpected expenses.

## Health and Emergency Services

Health and Emergency Services are crucial aspects to consider during your time in San Francisco. Here's what you need to know:

- Medical Facilities:

**Hospitals**: San Francisco has several renowned hospitals and medical centers that provide comprehensive healthcare services. Examples include UCSF Medical Center, California Pacific Medical Center, and Zuckerberg San Francisco General Hospital.

**Clinics**: There are numerous clinics and urgent care centers throughout the city, offering medical services for non-emergency situations. These are convenient for minor illnesses or injuries that do not require a hospital visit.

**Emergency Services**:

Dialing 911: In case of emergencies, dial 911 for immediate assistance from police, fire, or medical services.

Ambulance Services: San Francisco has a reliable ambulance service that can transport you to the nearest hospital in case of a medical emergency.

Fire Department: The San Francisco Fire Department plays a critical role in responding to fires, medical emergencies, and other incidents. They are well-equipped to handle various situations.

- Travel Insurance:

It is highly recommended to have travel insurance that covers medical expenses and emergency medical evacuation. This ensures you are financially protected in case of unexpected medical situations during your trip.

- Pharmacies:

Pharmacies and drugstores are readily available throughout the city, where you can purchase over-the-counter medications, personal care items, and prescription drugs.

- Vaccinations:

Check with your healthcare provider or travel clinic prior to your trip to ensure you are up to date on routine vaccinations. Depending on your travel plans, you may also need additional vaccinations.

- Safety Precautions:

It's important to take necessary safety precautions to minimize the risk of accidents or health issues. Be cautious when crossing streets, follow traffic rules, and use designated pedestrian crossings.

San Francisco's weather can vary, so dress appropriately and carry necessary items like sunscreen, hats, and umbrellas to protect yourself from the sun or rain.

Stay hydrated, especially on warmer days, and carry a reusable water bottle with you.

Practice good hygiene by washing your hands regularly, particularly before eating or handling food.

Important Contacts:

Emergency: Dial 911

Non-emergency Police Assistance: (415) 553-0123

Poison Control: (800) 222-1222

## Essential Packing List

Let's make sure you have everything you need for a fantastic trip! Here's a fun and friendly packing list to help you out:

- Weather-Appropriate Clothing:

**Layered clothing**: San Francisco's weather can be a bit unpredictable, so pack light layers that you can easily add or remove as needed. That way, you'll be prepared for any temperature changes!

**Sweater or jacket**: Even in the summer, San Francisco nights can get a little chilly. Bring a lightweight jacket or sweater to keep you cozy.

**Comfy walking shoes**: Get ready to conquer those famous San Francisco hills! Make sure to pack comfortable shoes that will keep your feet happy as you explore the city on foot.

- Travel Documents:

**Valid passport or ID:** Don't leave home without your identification documents, especially if you're an international traveler. We want to make sure you can breeze through security.

**Travel itinerary:** Keep track of your travel plans by having printed or digital copies of your flight tickets, hotel reservations, and any activities or tours you've booked in advance.

**Health insurance information:** It's always a good idea to have your health insurance card and any necessary medical documents with you, just in case.

- Electronics and Accessories:

**Phone and charger:** Your trusty smartphone will be your navigator, communicator, and memory-capturer during your trip. Don't forget to pack your charger too!

**Power adapter:** If you're coming from another country, remember to bring a power adapter so you can keep your devices charged and ready to go.

**Camera**: Get ready to capture all the iconic sights of San Francisco! Whether you have a dedicated camera or just your phone, don't miss those picture-perfect moments.

Personal Essentials:

**Toiletries**: Pack travel-sized toiletries like your toothbrush, toothpaste, shampoo, conditioner, and other personal care items you can't live without.

Medications: If you take any prescription medications, make sure to bring enough for your entire trip. It's better to be prepared!

**Sunscreen**: Protect your skin from the California sun! Don't forget to pack sunscreen, especially if you plan to spend time outdoors.

Basic first aid kit: It's always handy to have a small first aid kit with essentials like band-aids and pain relievers. Better safe than sorry!

- Money and Security:

**Wallet with ID and cards**: Keep your essential cards and identification in a safe and secure wallet or money belt. Let's keep your money matters in order!

**Cash**: It's always a good idea to have some cash on hand for smaller purchases, transportation, or places that might not accept cards.

**Travel lock:** Keep your belongings secure by using a travel lock on your luggage. Safety first!

- Miscellaneous:

Travel guidebook or maps: Plan your adventures with the help of a travel guidebook or access maps on your phone. Discover the best spots and hidden gems!

Reusable water bottle: Stay hydrated throughout the day by carrying a reusable water bottle and refilling it as needed. We don't want any dehydration during your explorations.

**Snacks**: Pack some tasty snacks to keep your energy up while you're out and about. Munch on the go and keep the adventure going!

Remember to tailor your packing list to your specific needs and planned activities. And don't forget to check the weather forecast before you go, so you'll be prepared for whatever San Francisco has in store for you. With a well-packed bag, you'll be all set for an amazing time in the city by the bay!

# Conclusion

As we wrap up this awesome tourist guide to San Francisco, it's important to keep in mind that we've only scratched the surface of this vibrant city's offerings. San Francisco is like a treasure trove, bursting with diversity, creativity, and a fascinating history. You're in for a real treat!

Sure, you've learned about the big guns like the Golden Gate Bridge, Alcatraz Island, and Fisherman's Wharf - they're classics for a reason. But here's the scoop: it's time to break free from the crowd! Take a chance and explore the lesser-known neighborhoods, cozy local eateries, and hip cultural hotspots that might not make it into every guidebook. Embrace the quirkiness and be ready to stumble upon some incredible surprises.

Here's a hot tip: mingle with the locals, chat up the awesome folks working at your hotel, and tap into their San Francisco expertise. They've got the inside scoop! Get ready for hidden gems, off-the-beaten-path attractions, and mouthwatering culinary delights that will blow your mind and make your adventure even more authentic.

Now, before you dive headfirst into your San Francisco escapade, remember to keep safety in mind. Just like any bustling city, it's important to stay sharp, be aware of your surroundings, and take those necessary precautions. Get acquainted with local customs, figure out the best way to get around, and jot down emergency contact info. Safety first, my friend!

As we bid you farewell, we want to send you off with our warmest wishes for an unforgettable stay in San Francisco. May your journey be filled with wonder, your encounters be filled with pure joy, and your memories be etched with the indelible spirit of this captivating city. So go on, embrace the enchantment of San Francisco, and create stories that'll have you grinning from ear to ear for years to come. Bon voyage, and have a blast!

Thank You!

Made in United States
Troutdale, OR
08/03/2023

11784252R00149